Smart Luck

& the seven other qualities of great entrepreneurs

Andrew Davidson

FINANCIAL TIMES
Prentice Hall

An imprint of Pearson Education
London / New York / San Francisco / Toronto / Sydney / Tokyo / Singapore
Hong Kong / Cape Town / Madrid / Paris / Milan / Munich / Amsterdam

PEARSON EDUCATION LIMITED

Head Office:
Edinburgh Gate
Harlow CM20 2JE
Tel: +44 (0)1279 623623
Fax: +44 (0)1279 431059

London Office:
128 Long Acre
London WC2E 9AN
Tel: +44 (0)20 7447 2000
Fax: +44 (0)20 7240 5771
Website: www.business-minds.com

First published in Great Britain in 2002

Photographs © Harry Borden/IPG

ISBN 0 273 65265 6

British Library Cataloguing in Publication Data
A CIP catalogue record for this book can be obtained from the British Library

10 9 8 7 6 5 4 3 2

Designed by Claire Brodmann Book Designs, Lichfield, Staffs
Typeset by Northern Phototypesetting Co. Ltd, Bolton
Printed and bound in Great Britain by Biddles Ltd, Guildford & King's Lynn

The Publishers' policy is to use paper manufactured from sustainable forests.

dedication

for ER and RI

contents

NORTH ACTON, LONDON

Dunstone has a way of like a kid

looking up at you
hoping for extra
pocket money

I AM SITTING IN AN ARMCHAIR IN A NONDESCRIPT OFFICE IN west London. It's raining outside, spattering the dismal car park that fills the concrete from office foyer to grey, congested road. Charlie Dunstone, a short, stubby young man with a face like a morose gerbil and a paper worth, at this time, of more than £200m, is fiddling with his mobile phone. He is giving me his girlfriend's number. I am interviewing him for a magazine and he is so relaxed, so at ease with himself that he doesn't mind who I want to talk to. People who know Dunstone respect him for that, almost more than his ability to make money.

His phone is slim and steel, the size of a credit card. It rings while he is searching. He answers it.

"Are you on your mo, Mark? I'll call you back," he says.

Charlie Dunstone

Mos are his business. Since he set up his Carphone Warehouse retail chain with £6,000 in savings, it has grown to straddle the booming market for mobile phones in Europe. On the day we are talking, he is still only 34.

How much is the phone worth?

Dunstone's face, haloed in blond, spikey hair, suddenly beams. He has a way of looking up at you like a kid hoping for extra pocket money. He cups the phone lightly in his hand.

"Oh it's just come out," he says. "It costs £299, but it's probably not worth that."

You can't say that! Your customers are buying it…

He grins.

"Yes I can. I'd say that to someone. But if you are absolutely determined to have the very latest and the very smallest, then…"

His little eyes twinkle.

When people ask Charlie Dunstone why he has been so successful, he likes to crack a joke. "I'm the luckiest man since Ringo Starr," he says.

What makes any entrepreneur successful?

The smart ones say luck. But, of course, it's more than just that…

NURTURED NATURE

We don't need that crap.

We can be casual.
We can be Branson

In a Greek nightclub

Richard Branson wants to say something. I can tell. He has that look which bosses get when they deal with journalists day in, day out – a faint hesitation of calculation before they open their mouths.

We are standing in an Athens nightclub, way past midnight, sometime in spring, 1993. I've been sent by a newspaper colour supplement to shadow him, to tag along and write an extended profile examining his character, his popularity, his determination to overcome all odds. It is a key time in Branson's career. He has just emerged victorious in his mud-slinging battle with British Airways, winning a large sum in libel damages and a public apology from his arch-enemy Lord King, the BA chairman. (Forget the fact that, later, people would dispute the money, the victory, the tactics.)

King, a seasoned, old-style corporate chief – self-made man who rode to hounds, lord at Margaret Thatcher's round table – has already tried to explain his mishandling of the fight thus: "If Richard Branson had worn a pair of steel-rimmed glasses, a double-breasted suit and shaved off his beard, I would have taken him seriously. As it was, I couldn't... I underestimated him."

It is a prescient moment. Branson, the jumper-wearing beardie, has finally been confirmed as Britain's best-loved businessman. Within seven years no-one is wearing suits – the dotcommers, the start-ups, the agency people, the consultants, venture capitalists, even accountants. By 2000, you would underestimate someone if they *were* wearing a suit (must be a lawyer). We don't need that crap any more. We can be casual. We can be Branson.

Branson had won, he had overturned the forces of fusty, old-style capitalism by proving that malevolent powers lurked underneath. And he had managed to make us all feel sorry for a man worth, in 1993, £475m, with huge houses in Holland Park and Oxfordshire, an island in the Caribbean, swimming pools, Jacuzzis, tennis courts, cricket pitches and hundreds of not particularly well-paid employees. Sorry for him, because BA had not played fair, they had rigged their computers to steal his customers, engaged private eyes to dig up dirt, tried to smear and besmirch his reputation. And because we like Branson, because he is different, because, in some small way, he changed how business is done and perceived, and because deep down we want to be him. If Britbiz was a movement, he would probably have been its founder.

Back to the nightclub. It had been a long and pretty hellish day, traipsing round after the man as he did whatever you do on these kind of whirlwind foreign tours. Attended a party thrown by the British Consul, flew out to the island of Hydra in his helicopter to check a potential hotel site, out to dinner with a party so big a whole restaurant is annexed. The main purpose of the trip is to launch Branson's new joint venture with a small Greek airline, which as far as I could understand was repainting its planes, changing its name to Virgin, dressing its stewardesses in Virgin red, flying between Gatwick and Athens, and paying Branson handsomely for the privilege. Nice work if you can get it. Branson is in town on the inaugural flight to pump up publicity – something he is truly an expert in – accompanied by his wife, his kids, his parents, umpteen Virgin staff, travel agents, trade journalists, a documentary TV crew and me.

And he handles it all beautifully, giving time for everyone, making the right speeches at the right moment in that rather winning, hesitant manner he has, as if everything he has to say comes right from the heart, as if he is a bit embarrassed about it, and as if, erm, gosh, er, no-one has ever, um, asked him to speak in, erm, public before. And after the restaurant his family are sent back to the hotel and we all pile into the nightclub. Half of Athens seems to be inside, convinced that Branson is bringing Sting and Phil Collins with him (no-one told them he sold the record company the year before). The other half of Athens is queueing outside.

Inside the club it is surreal. A large screen plays a Virgin Atlantic corporate video. On a small stage opposite a quartet of ageing musicians is playing a loud bossa nova. Every so often one of them leans into the microphone and choruses Virgeen! Virgeen! Branson, in white shirt and jeans, is watching from a balcony above. A Virgin PR dances on a table next to him and a coterie of red-jacketed flight attendants, who have followed him like an amiable posse all trip, stand waiting.

I stick close to Branson, looking to add colour for my piece, knowing that colour is what he is good at providing (before anyone else in business, he saw that wave coming, and rode it brilliantly). I can see he feels my presence – I might write he feels my need, but that could be misconstrued – and eventually he tries to oblige. Squashed against a back wall in the club, flanked by fans, he turns to me and grins.

"Hey, did you ever have a little black book, you know, one where you keep all your girlfriends' addresses?"

I am hopeless at macho banter. I can't think how to respond. No, I reply, fumbling my cue. His face clouds fleetingly. Branson, who at that stage in his career, was always making jokes about being an incorrigible flirt, had been aiming for a point of contact and missed. What could he have been about to say? Probably just some good copy, finely judged to look personal. He does it all the time, and I'd muffed it.

The funny thing was, by far the most interesting person on that trip was not Branson himself, but his mother.

Two questions

Many years later, perched on the edge of an expensive seat in a vast luxury flat in London's West End, I ask Sir Alan Sugar, boss of Amstrad, consumer electronics king, self-made man incarnate, what makes a good entrepreneur? He answers swiftly, aggressively, uncompromisingly.

"It's the way you are born, what's in you, brain power, fast brain, aptitude for business you are in, quick understanding of what can be done and what can't be done, watching the way markets change, jumping in quickly and exploiting them, and having a sense of what the end-user wants."

It begs two questions. Could there be a gene for entrepreneurial activity? And what kind of upbringing produces entrepreneurs?

... your mum and dad

I have lost count of the amount of times I have sat in a room with a successful man telling me about how close he was to his mother. I didn't twig till Anita Roddick, the founder of The Body Shop, told me about her dad. Her real dad, not the man who had been married to her mother. It was complicated, difficult, not the sort of thing you would wish on any child growing up, but what came through, apart from the sense of her knowing long before she was told, was the bond.

Mothers and sons, fathers and daughters. Perhaps it comes down to confidence, to removing that fear of rejection. A parent who tells a child all things are possible, whatever anyone else says or feels, to push on regardless, not to doubt that they will be loved whatever happens, may well produce egomaniacal monsters for the world, but also a fair proportion of confident leaders, maybe even some great business builders. That's not nature at work – how many successful entrepreneurs are children of successful entrepreneurs? – but nurture. Or at least, some cunning combination of the two.

> *Nature: ...the inherent power or force by which physical and mental activities are sustained; the inherent dominating power or impulse (in people or animals) by which action or character is determined, directed or controlled; (opp. nurture) heredity as an influence on or determinant of personality ...*(OXFORD ENGLISH DICTIONARY)
>
> *Nurture: ...the process of bringing up or training a person, esp. a child; tutelage; fostering care. Also, social environment as an influence on or determinant of personality (opp. nature).*
> (OXFORD ENGLISH DICTIONARY)

Bringing up Richard

Eve Branson. Thin, blonde, good-looking, even in her 70s. If you read the biographies, she is regularly said to have given Branson his ambition – Ted, his genial, erudite, barrister dad (son of a judge, grandson of a colonial lawyer), gave him his charm. Talk to Branson and he will say that it was Eve (father a stockbroker, grandmother secretary to the Bishop of Edinburgh, grandfather a clergyman) who forced the shy boy out of himself, who stopped him watching television and loafing about, who forced him to *do* things, to perform at parties, to get outside, to get noticed. Most famously, she was the mother who dropped him off, aged four, half a mile from home, and told him to find his own way back. To toughen him up.

Branson once remarked: "My parents brought me up with this philosophy: 'You must do things – you mustn't watch what other people are doing; you mustn't listen to what other people are doing'."

It's as if she unburdened him of the self-consciousness that holds the rest of Britain back. Perform, cross-dress, hang from a helicopter, balloon around the world, get noticed, be brave. You've nothing to lose except my affection if you don't… *perform*. Eve was a dancer from a well-off family who worked rather than loafed. She became an air hostess. She ran her own embroidery business from the back garden. She kept notes and diaries. Sound familiar? She is also an immensely strong personality.

I met her on that trip to Athens. She and Ted were almost ancillary Virgin executives, clucking over the press, partying with the best of them, but never exchanging more than polite banalities. Branson had his wife Joan and children Holly and Sam with him too. Joan, famously, never gives

Richard Branson

on the most

interviews but will chat cautiously. It was extraordinarily confident of Branson to push his whole family under the spotlight with that kind of pressure on them – some would find it distasteful. But we weren't there to write about them, and generally didn't. It was a very winning, or calculated, exercise in trust. The press took their cues from the Virgin staff. They were always edgy round Eve and Joan, trying to anticipate their needs, constantly prepared to back off.

The flight back to London was at 8am; Branson had kept the press pack partying till 4am. At the airport, Ted, white hair swept back, a Kipling volume in his summer suit pocket, approached a journalist sitting on the floor, hung over and groaning. "My, my," he grinned, "you look like Atlas carrying the world on his shoulders." Eve, meanwhile, resplendent in black stretch suit and gold trim, was starting to write notes furiously on her Virgin press pack. Later I was told she was preparing a book about her travels with Richard. Her son, it transpired, was pulling out all the stops to prevent her from finding a publisher.

founded his whole career
phenomenal PR
known to man

Richard Branson

The art of profile

By the year 2000, British business – funky, sexy, Cool Britannia business, the sort of hiphoppy biz vibe that says it's neat to trade shares on the net, set up on your own and *create* wealth – has learnt from Branson.

Luke Johnson, one of the brighter entrepreneurs around, says to me: "Is it important to have profile? It's not important, it's not essential, but it can be helpful. Lots of people say, keep a low profile. The obvious argument against that is Richard Branson who has founded his whole career on the most phenomenal PR known to man. He's had good people and good ideas but it is the profile that has carried him. I'm not saying he isn't a genius at it. What I am saying is, without the PR, he wouldn't be the richest self-made man in the UK. That's the great counter-argument to those who say, never get publicity."

Luke Johnson, on top of making tens of millions of pounds from his investments in restaurant chains such as Pizza Express and Belgo, writes his own newspaper column.

Branson the hero

When he was growing up, Richard Branson was told that being shy was being selfish.

Can the world ever get it right about Branson? We don't know him, we don't live with him, we didn't have his upbringing. We can only make stabs in the dark that sometimes draw blood.

Tom Bower's biography of Branson sits on my desk. You might call it a brilliant book of bile, comparable only to Albert Goldman's work on John Lennon and Elvis Presley, studies in sadistic scholarship. Is that too strong? I don't think so. Yet Bower's book is a timely antidote to the other Branson biographies; you can read them side by side, yin and yang, Branson the brave adventurer, Branson the cheating philanderer (male entrepreneurs and oversized libidos: discuss). Even if it is a fair and accurate appraisal – and Bower's book certainly rings true, the mugs who lost their ideas to Branson, the gullible staff who worked for pennies while the boss salted his millions away off-shore, the convoluted, contradictory doublespeak of the PR-obsessed tycoon – no-one wants to hear that particular kind of truth. We prefer the truth we bought earlier. Branson the hero.

Because we've invested too much in it. And then, in 2000, the government refused to give him the National Lottery. If this is just about the only time that events have turned on Branson, the publicity bubble pricked, then what are we left with? Another deflated tycoon? But from where I am sitting, the bubble hasn't really burst, just sagged a bit and then swelled out again with renewed confidence. If that's your best shot….

Maybe it will just be a slow puncture.

I asked Branson once whether he enjoyed courting publicity. He shrugged. "You know," he said, "it's not that enjoyable when you do the same 15 interviews every day…" Then he gave me a jumble of thoughts disguised in his normal, stuttering, stop-start style.

"Well, there are two big dividing lines, you will never see anything with me that is family related, like Hello! magazine spreads, but if you are proud of the business you have to get out there and promote it. The only business I will ever do interviews about is the airline. We get approached regularly and always say no to anything that doesn't put the airline name in the forefront. Now, having got the name Virgin well-known worldwide, either I can sit back as chairman and say I am not interested in working any more, or I can be proud of the project I have launched and work bloody hard to make sure it is a success, and support all the people that are working hard on the ground to make it work."

Also, he says, ticking off the advantages, a high profile makes a boss's work easier. "Because I am well-known I can pick up a phone to anyone in the world and get straight through to the president of a company and get things done."

In other words, he'd thought it all out. And he is quite at ease being in the spotlight, just like the boy who was dragged downstairs to perform for his mother's guests. Being shy, he was told, is being selfish. Does that define his management style too? Make him more overbearing, more patriarchal, perhaps?

"I guess I am more patriarchal than a lot of bosses. There are little things, like I ask the staff to write to me with suggestions which, in a conventional business, people would be worried about bypassing their managers. I think because people come straight to me, I have taken on the role of head of the union – oh, this is going to sound awful in print – but I often think that if there is a need for a union, then management has failed. It's usually set up in frustration at the decisions made. If everyone in the company can go straight to me, then I will give them the benefit of the doubt over their managers, and managers accept that approach. I will usually side with the individual to make sure there is no frustration bubbling up. I will mediate between the two."

Does he think he is more pivotal to the business than other kinds of bosses, because there is more focus on him? "I suspect that's the case but you have to differentiate between the different kinds of businesses. I have a hands-on approach to the travel business because the only way I can see it succeeding is like private enterprise where the owner is hands-on, like a club or a restaurant, the personal touch. To compete with the big companies you have that quality, where the person at the top is concerned with much of the attention to detail…"

What will happen to Branson? Some who know him have always said his popularity contains the seed of its own destruction. "He has a very perceptive view of what attracts people to buy his products," says Sir

Michael Bishop, boss of rival airline British Midland, "but he will have to recognize the moment at which people tire of the image. That's the great trap." Others think that, just as he has made more people interested in entrepreneurialism, so his particular way of doing business will eventually be picked apart. "He will go down," says one venture capitalist who had his fingers burnt dealing with Branson. "I absolutely predict it."

And yet we are still waiting. Even the calamitous performance of Virgin trains hasn't pricked his bubble. Sure, the articles where Branson takes the writer ballooning or to his summer party or off on a plane do look a little tired now, exercises in evasion rather than insight. But his ads still carry his face, he is still his company's most potent marketing tool. My osteopath has read every book on Branson. People are obsessed. Branson is confident enough, it seems, to have no private side at all. What makes a man do that? Because it works.

And sitting in Branson's opulent home in London's Holland Park, with its landscaped gardens and basement swimming pool and conservatory the size of most of his employees' houses, I remember feeling rather confused. This is not a home. It's crawling with office staff. The joke in Virgin went that, every so often, Joan made Branson move to another house to regain some private space, before the workforce encroached again.

And as Branson is the most influential British business figure of his generation, close almost to blocking out the sun, where is that taking us?

15–0

A woman I play tennis with said to me last year: "I read about you on holiday. You're in Richard Branson's autobiography. It quite spoiled my trip." She laughs. For just a moment Branson's shadow had widened even further to engulf me too.

If

In the end you have to admit – Branson is a glorious boy. It struck me after spending those days with him: he is surrounded by women, women who adore him, strong women who organize him, his wife Joan, his mother Eve, women who idolize him. Yet none has a position of power in his business empire. He is the lovable, calculating tyke who never understood girls and never had to grow up and wear a suit, whose mum always tousled his hair when he came back from school with rotten exam results and said, never mind Richard, I still love you, just make a mark, be different to the rest. He could do no wrong even when he did wrong.

Could you set out to bring up Richard? As builders say, two chances (might work, might not). Yet, somehow, something seemed to freeze-dry him at age 18, stumbling into adulthood, his ambition and drive and determination overcoming boyish gaucheness and intellectual insecurity. Having watched him work, I once wrote that Branson ran his businesses like a feudal lord, despatching orders from his dining room table (literally), his loyal retainers stepping over the wolfhounds (metaphorically) to reach him. But looking back and reading the books and watching what's happened to him, he now seems more and more like a character from Lindsay Anderson's If.

Malcolm McDowell, shy-boy-turned-cocky-chancer, decides not to shoot up the school but go into business, and run it his way. A gang of (male) mates to plot with. The occasional chick to dance by the juke box. Someone to sort your clothes out. Someone to take their clothes off. People to take advantage of. Money to be made. Increasingly embattled but always cocksure.

Or maybe the key to Branson is that, from a distance, he is fantastically unthreatening. That's why people like him, why they want to join his gang, and why rivals underestimate him, just as Lord King did, just as so many competitors and business partners have in the past. They think they can easily be as smart and gung-ho and full-of-fun. They think they can adopt that character. I wonder.

Two facts

In my line of work, bosses invariably ascribe their dominant characteristics, those characteristics that have made them successful, to one or other parent. Men mostly to their mothers. Women to their fathers. Generally, too – and remember, these are men and women who are now very rich compared with you and me – they talk about childhoods where money was tight, where parents fussed over their lack of cash, where financial crisis was always imminent, or indeed upon them.

Most people believe successful business leaders are just products of their environment.

```
To: Andrew Davidson, 101457,2115
Date: Wed, Oct 4, 2000, 2:35 pm
RE: Mandrake - 10 October 2000



Dear Guest,

The next Mandrake will be held on Tuesday 10 October 2000 at the usual
venue, the bar above PizzaExpress, 23 Bruton Place, Mayfair W1 at 6.30pm.

Our speaker will be Jacqueline de Baer, Founder and Chief Executive of de
Baer, which designs, manufactures and distributes corporate clothing.  The
Company was established in 1984 on a beach in Spain and now employs over 70
staff and has a list of blue-chip clients including Marriott Hotels, Boots
Opticians, Odeon and JMC.

Please reply to this email to let us know whether you will be attending.

We look forward to seeing you next week.

Kind regards,

Luke Johnson & David Ross
```

Mandrake e-invite

Luke Johnson invites me to the Mandrake Club (but only because I asked)

It's quite easy to like Luke Johnson, not just because he is prepared to say yes, but also because he is, when he wants to be, a funny and caustic interviewee. You might also enjoy the fact that many journalists mistrust him, can't quite make him out. They hate the fact that his father is one of their own and Luke himself – with that weekly column in a national newspaper – is not a bad scribbler. It's as if Johnson himself is saying, I can make millions and do your job in my spare time... Johnson is too bright to be a Branson. Too threatening.

I'm not sure Johnson likes me. He says I can come to the Mandrake, the monthly entrepreneurs' club that he set up with Charlie Dunstone's number two, David Ross, if I follow Salisbury Club rules. What are those? No quotes, few details. Well, OK.

The club has an aura around it, Johnson doesn't like journalists coming, the tabloids whisper that only millionaires are invited. Oh please. In fact, it's a few youngish people standing round plates of cut-up pizza listening to an entrepreneur speak. If the speaker's fun, it works; if not, then it's low-key. But it's a sign of the times that such a gathering can get others begging for invites. Being an entrepreneur is suddenly cool. People want money, people want independence, they want things for themselves. Johnson, like Branson before him, has become a little bit of an icon.

When I turn up one autumn night to the second floor room above Pizza Express off Berkeley Square, Johnson doesn't recognize me. I shake his hand, introduce myself and he says, I want to talk to you later. I'd just published a long profile of Johnson and his tone is that of a man who wants to put me straight on a few things.

That night he had invited Jacqueline de Baer to speak. De Baer, good looking, charmingly informal, in her 40s, has made millions setting up a

Being an entrepreneur

People want money,

corporate clothing firm. She started with swimming trunks for holiday reps and broadened the range till she was mass-producing for supermarket staff and rail employees. She explains how she is dealing almost more in motivation than overalls now. We nod and sip our beers. There are around 40 of us gathered to listen. We've already attacked the subsidized bar – £1.50 for a Perroni, thanks, Luke. Then we listen to de Baer's 15-minute speech, how she made it, what drives her on. At one point she says, "I'm not quite sure why I am doing this tonight, it's my birthday!" Everyone laughs.

After a few questions about where the business is going next, we return to the bar. A gaggle of men hang around, mostly young, mostly loud, ties off, hands in pockets, quite a few, I would guess, in advertising or other client service businesses. Johnson, 38, thin, good-looking with dark eyes and an upturned nose, moves from group to group, chatting sociably like a night club owner in his black T-shirt and jacket.

is suddenly cool.

people want

independence

I ask him why he does it. He says he needed to pick up on the entrepreneurial buzz sweeping London. "It was an idea of Rosso and mine, great fun, we just wanted to have great people. We've had Ken Bates, Peter Stringfellow, William Hague, Alan Sugar, Christopher Bland… We're pretty discriminating about who we invite, it's all off the record and we try to get as many entrepreneurs as possible." No-one gets an easy ride. The questions to Jeffrey Archer, when he spoke, were "pretty assertive", says Johnson. The funny thing is, he adds, that while lots of people know about the club, most are too shy to approach him about it. He giggles. "I think they think it's a secret club like Hellfire or something."

There are other reasons too, I would guess. Johnson enjoys being at the centre of attention and likes organizing things, but is hardly the most approachable of men. He has an acid tongue and you don't have to go far in London to find people in business who have fallen foul of it. One I spoke to, working for a rival restaurant operation, fulminated against Johnson to

Luke Johnson

me, accusing him of claiming credit for other people's success (Pizza Express) and arguing that he is totally motivated by his rivalry with his once best friend, pubs entrepreneur Hugh Osmond.

And that's probably true. But it still doesn't explain why Johnson wants to spin other entrepreneurs around him. Is he frightened of missing a trick? Is he constantly on the look-out for ideas to borrow? When I ask him, Johnson says that when he was young, he always had little projects on the go, that's what differentiated him from the rest of the family. Getting teams together for sports, and organizing projects. "I like that word that was used in the sixteenth or seventeenth century," he says. "Projectors, people who have projects. I didn't see it that way at the time, but I see it now, I always liked organizing." The Mandrake Club is just another little project.

"And the great thing about clubs is that you meet interesting people," says Johnson. And people, and the opportunities for business that they provide, are what pushes a man like Johnson on.

Cold hand Luke

Johnson, worth £80m-odd at one stage in 2000, describes himself as "an entrepreneur, of sorts, not in the classic definition, but in the sense I work for myself and don't work for salary".

He made his money out of a variety of investments – but principally that stake in the Pizza Express restaurant chain which he bought into and expanded in the early 90s. Since then he has moved on to another restaurant business, Belgo, which also owns up-market eateries such as Le Caprice and The Ivy, and investments in internet start-ups and technology funds. But of more interest is how he networks. He knows people, he is connected, his name pops up in the most unexpected of places. A bit like his father Paul Johnson, one-time socialist and now celebrated right-wing columnist for the *Daily Mail* and a man who moves easily among industrialists and politicians. His mother, on the other hand, is a former Labour Party activist turned counsellor, and widely praised for her sweet nature. Luke Johnson, according to those who've worked with him, missed out on that.

But actually he is a man of contrasts. One minute glacially cold, the next warm and friendly, a wit with a volcanic temper, a voracious bookworm who amasses money but spurns the trappings of wealth – apart from property. He likes to keep little flats in all his favourite cities, New York, Paris, Edinburgh, Brighton, which he often lends out to friends. But he likes to travel by public transport and plays his tennis on public courts. "He really doesn't like losing, though," according to one friend.

He also appears to be a character on the cusp of great things: either high achievement or disaster. There is the whiff of danger about him, about what he does, how he does it. Some mistrust him. "He's too sharp," one national newspaper editor told me. When I put this to Johnson, he spun it back in the form of a question about Nigel Wray, the financier and property developer, who shares his predilection for making big profits using shell companies.

Do people think Wray is sharp?

Yes.

Well, he says, there is a word for what they feel. Envy.

Where was Johnson's thirst for success honed? In his large and competitive family, he says. One of four children, Johnson is the third son.

"My father is an ambitious individual, he set the tone," says Johnson. The family were brought up to be high achievers. Johnson's eldest brother works on the Daily Telegraph, his middle brother is a carpenter, his younger sister works in television.

"I took my ambition, and a little bit of temper, from my father, my ability to make friends from my mum. I think we were quite a volatile family in terms of mood, quite excitable. Someone said to me the other day, when we had just witnessed a piece of bad behaviour, what kind of upbringing did they have? But I think you do get permission to behave like that by witnessing it."

But temper, he goes on to argue, is no bad thing. "Generally I prefer it to being too calm. Give me someone who is making a difference rather than staying relaxed because he doesn't want to get worked up. You don't go into business if you want to relax and have a stress-free life. I think people who go on about how bad stress is for you are full of shit, frankly. You see these people who die a year after retiring and think: it was probably stress that was keeping them alive!"

And the urge to make money?

"I don't think I have a flair with numbers, no-one in my family has, you just get it through practice. I was looking for areas to excel in. I was not going to go into mainstream journalism and writing, though I probably could have as writing comes naturally to me, one of the reasons why I do a newspaper column…

"My parents never had a lot of money, but my dad's always been a saver, a bit of a worrier about money. He has been very well paid, among one of the better paid writers, but he is quite tough, he won't do work if he doesn't get well paid or doesn't want to do it, he's never been a hack, he's hardworking, he earns well, and has never been extravagant. He's part of the post-war generation that is conservative in its spending habits. That rubbed off somewhat, I always keep relatively low personal overheads. Anyway, spending money takes time, especially to spend and enjoy it, and if you are busy you don't have the time. And for people like me my money is my working capital. If I have spent it I have nothing to invest!"

Johnson's friends tell me he is obsessive about waste, costs and cash. It defines his business style. "And he is probably a bit risk-averse", says one, "hence the portfolio of interests. He is also shy, and doesn't like confrontation, but he has this powerful personality and uses it to browbeat people."

Johnson says he made his first fortune through luck, but it was clearly smart luck. He had tried different careers after Oxford; ad-man (six months), Jonathan Aitken's assistant (one year), media analyst (three years), investment adviser (one year) before going it alone, always on the sniff for opportunities.

It was that sniffing – a chance ad in the *Financial Times* in 1990 which led to a contact who later gave him a tip – that culminated in the deal that made his name, a complex merger that allowed a vehicle co-owned by Johnson and his Oxford pal, Hugh Osmond, to get hold of Pizza Express, a well-liked but under-performing restaurant chain.

"It was luck," says Johnson again. "In 1993 the small companies market had a revival, the country came out of recession and the restaurant sector began to boom. And we bought a great business that had huge untapped potential. It is very rare you get hold of a great brand that has not been fully exploited. It had been going since 1965 with a heritage that we took advantage of." They pushed the brand, introduced new efficiencies, expanded the product. It all worked.

And shrunk the pizzas? (I, like many other Pizza Express fans, really do believe that Johnson shrunk the pizzas). "No," he says with that smile, "we did it without shrinking the pizzas or changing the product in any way."

Making connections with Matthew Freud

I am interested in connections. Writing a piece about Mike Edelson, the Mancunian financier who supplies shell companies for in-a-hurry entrepreneurs, I get talking to PR boss Matthew Freud. Edelson had grilled me about Luke Johnson. I got the impression he wanted to meet him, maybe to sell to him. Freud says: "Oh no, they have met, at my house, for dinner, I introduced them." The connections are going on all the time, furiously. That's why the newpaper columns are valuable to Johnson. He is out there, he is a face. From time to time, he says, he gets a phone call from someone who has read something. "People phone me up and most people enjoy talking about themselves, sometimes it has useful spin-offs."

And sometimes it doesn't. What Johnson didn't tell me back then was that the BBC had persuaded him to appear in its series *Back To The Floor*, where bosses take on menial jobs in their own companies. He spent days being filmed working at Belgo Centraal, his company's flagship West End restaurant. He manned the door, shouted orders, peeled onions. The programme, eventually screened in November 2000, showed staff showering him with a litany of complaints about pay and conditions, until at one stage, over the onions, confronted by a prolonged whinge from a chef, Johnson tore off his microphone and stomped up to the chief executive's office. He returned later, though who knows after what discussions with the programme makers.

I only agreed to do this, Johnson kept telling the camera, because I thought it would be good publicity for Belgo (the only reason any boss ever appears in these programmes, of course).

It takes a special kind of personality to manage the media. It has to be in your nature.

A digression on publicity: Stelios Haji-Ioannou

Stelios, the Greek-born entrepreneur who founded EasyJet and likes to be known by his first name, is a Branson fan. He has marketed his businesses obsessively through a cultivation of his own image. He is the brand, he is the human face of his business, he is interviewed endlessly because of our growing obsession with entrepreneurs, and he likes to talk about himself as the underdog, champion of people's causes. He also likes stunts, and forbids his staff from wearing ties. All this he has learnt from Branson.

He too is the child of an affluent upbringing. In his case, far more affluent than Branson, as his father is a Greek-Cypriot shipping millionaire. No financial crises in his youth, you suspect (hmm, which boat shall I take out this weekend? I'm just not sure…). But there is, he said once, no affection between him and his dad, as there never is between father and son in Greece. Really? We need to know more, but he is not saying. His early life, like other parts of the Stelios landscape, remains curiously sparse, as if someone has just emptied the room before troublesome visitors arrive.

Stelios is also clever, and a graduate of the London School of Economics where, you suspect, he probably read up furiously on entrepreneurialism. He too allows a constant but only partial view of his life, but it seems as

Stelios doesn't think

suitable to appear in

empty as his soulless flat in Monte Carlo where he lives, the most soulless town in Europe. With Stelios, the man tipped to be even bigger than Branson, you always feel something is missing.

I spent much of 2000 chasing him for an interview. A men's mag asked me to write a piece about him. I rang up Stelios's in-house PR man; he was polite but harassed, though he seemed enthusiastic about the idea of yet another interview. He invited me to watch his boss give interviews to the BBC for their Budget Day Special from the EasyGroup's internet cafe in London's Victoria. Stelios was to add the entrepreneur's viewpoint. All of a sudden, that was important.

When I got there it was pandemonium. The place was packed with punters – backpackers, students – plugging away at the screens and keyboards. Exhausted cafe staff stepped over the wires and cables laid out by the TV crews for their coverage. The place looked grimey and abused, as if a bunch of moonlighting chippies had put it together in a hurry, barely managing to

a men's glossy is for his more serious image

maybe

bitter

being

am just
at
jilted

Stelios Haji-Ioannou

clear up afterwards. At the back of the store a BBC crew fretted over some kind of outside broadcast console. Downstairs, in a cavernous basement equally packed with students and backpackers, Stelios, looking rotundly preppy in suit and casual shirt, was giving an interview to an American TV crew. The PR man stood anxiously by.

As I introduced myself, a BBC producer butted in. He was well-spoken and brusquely agitated, confident in the priority of his own work, maybe his own existence.

"Where's Stelios?" he barked, not even apologizing for leaning in.

Over there, said the PR man, smiling faintly.

"What's he doing?"

An interview for American TV.

"What? I am not sure we like that." Then he swore, scowled and spun back up the stairs without so much as an explanation. That, I thought, is what you have to get used to as an entrepreneur's PR man, the price of being available to the media.

I empathized.

In fact I was wasting my emotions. Over the next two months I endlessly asked for, and was promised, interview time with the chubby Greek genius whose empire – budget airline, internet cafés, car hire – seemed to be expanding every week. The magazine's editor tried too, but it was like lifting jelly. Stelios might, then he couldn't, might, then he couldn't again.

Eventually I asked the PR man. Is there a problem? He said, yes, there is, Stelios doesn't think a men's glossy is a suitable magazine to appear in, not good for his new, more serious image. But if you want to do it for a business magazine… When I told the editor, he said fuck it, I don't want to give any more publicity to the *** ***** anyway. But do it for someone else if you want.

So I went through the whole process again. Yes, definitely, if you're here, no, he's there, maybe, not sure, hang on, just gotta come last-minute. Sure, like I'm going to spend my life waiting for the call?

Eventually, as the flotation of EasyJet approached in late November 2000, the demands from EasyJet changed. We don't want you to interview Stelios, we want you to interview his head of operations. Suddenly Stelios wasn't important any more, too much Stelios, we must have publicity for the team.

It would be laughable if it wasn't so cack-handed. Then a firm of financial PRs, engaged for the float, got involved. They were smoothly emollient, wanting to provide Stelios (and maybe a few other clients as well, the usual piggybacking). But the dates never stacked up, they couldn't provide Stelios in time for a November issue, and they didn't want to do it any later than that because that was his float date. That was what he was selling. It was his agenda, perfectly understandable, but I began to feel persecuted as the only writer in the world who couldn't get to see the EasyJet boss. Bad PR. By autumn I had given up.

Later in the winter, riding an exercise bike in my local gym and gazing at the telly, sound off, dance music booming, I watched a silent episode of *Through The Keyhole*. Characterless flat in Monaco, a few Greek records lying around, an Economist. Something clicked. Stelios!, I screamed at the screen. Stelios! I don't know if the team got it, I couldn't hear, but eventually there he is, leaning against his balcony railing, his Mr Potato head bobbing in time to the yachts in the background. No time for me, but lots of time for the bloody *Through The Keyhole* team.

Of course, that's smart. Daytime television viewers are going to buy a lot more budget airline tickets than me, maybe even a lot more EasyJet shares. Yet it made me realize what a smooth publicity operation Branson runs, what mystique he developed, what charisma, what carapace – perhaps because he fell into it naturally, rather than developed a style because it worked for others.

So do I mean it was his nature, or have I already argued it was his nurture? Is the fact that Branson is "a natural" the reason he has done so much better than most? Will Stelios supersede him in our affections? I don't know. But with Stelios – so far – you always feel that something is missing.

Risk-free life

Maybe I am just bitter at being jilted.

"There is too much chippiness around," says Luke Johnson in that defiantly unposh accent he cultivates.

Really?

"I'm using it to describe middle-class people who are chippy about others with ambition."

Back to *sharp* again. But aren't people just more interested in how people make money now?

"Sure, the interest in entrepreneurialism has been growing for the past 20 years, the recent dot.com mania is just the latest version. People are more interested in money thanks to the decline in church and patriotism and other things, more interested in materialism. Yunno, you can give it the dinner party test. If you sat in a west London bourgeois dinner party 15 years ago, people would ask you what you did and then go, oo-er. Now they are rather more intrigued.

Do you go to a lot of dinner parties?

"No, I don't get invited that much actually."

In interview you can always feel Johnson's anger simmering gently, like a slow-cook pot of chilli, just out of reach.

When I ask him about nature or nurture, the influences that create the money-making entrepreneur, the ability to take risks, the urges, he talks about class.

"I went to a local grammar and primary school. Because I have never been to public school, there is more of a dividing line. I come from an educated family, but I always had friends who lived in council houses, only had one car, always holidayed in the UK, though I also knew people in posh houses. We were the media professional class, and I always considered my family to be middle class."

Is that important?

"I think where you were educated is very important in terms of where you can get to in society, and how much financial backing you can get. But accent and manners and who your tailor is, all that is being torn down because of the Lloyd's debacle or the internet generation or whatever. What's very important is your confidence level."

The key thing about the middle class, he goes on, is that they get trapped. Several things trap them, he says, "such as public school fees, they have partners who say, 'you're not taking our children out of school to fund your silly dotcom start-up', so they've got to keep working in the City or at Price Waterhouse or wherever, even though those start-ups could earn them more eventually. They choose a risk-free life."

Cambridge billionaire, fireman's son

Another view: three months earlier, sitting in a bland office at a bland PR company somewhere in a bland road off Marylebone High Street, Dr Mike Lynch, founder of Autonomy and Britain's first internet billionaire, had put the same thing differently.

The eldest of two boys (his younger brother is a builder), Lynch says he gets his work rate from his dad, a fireman, and his vision from his mum, a former intensive care nurse. "We didn't have much money, but she read a lot of books and when we got a car, we would go out every weekend, go and see museums, planes and steam engines. There would always be something interesting to do."

His father, he adds, is pretty much the sensible one, a great believer in 'you reap what you sow'. He also gave him what he took to be indispensable advice from a fireman: don't get a job that involves running into burning buildings. Lynch likes that joke. He tells it a lot.

"Both my parents were bright," he says, adopting a more serious tone, "and I suspect they did not have the opportunities to fulfil things that they could have done."

But the key was that, when it came to choosing careers, he never thought of plumping for the safe bet. It's not about how he was brought up, just about the environment around him. So many people he met at university switched tack to become solicitors and accountants and management consultants because those were the people they had grown up with, that was their milieu. "But one of the reasons I ended up where I am today," says Lynch, "is that I didn't know what a solicitor or accountant did! We didn't have any in my family or social circle."

Lynch, it should be noted, was a scholarship boy at a public school, his fees paid by his local authority; Johnson, a relatively well-off pupil at a state school with no fees to pay at all.

"If you've been in a class of 11-plus boys from Ilford and Redbridge at a public school," chortles Lynch, "you tend to learn how to duck and dive quickly."

In other words, it's not just what you are confronted with. It's how you respond to it.

SOFT RESILIENCE

You have to bounce

would say, OK,

back when the rest
enough

Expectations

Entrepreneurs, they say, break rules. So do criminals, of course, and we lock them up. Let's express it more accurately. Entrepreneurs confound expectations. And they don't buckle under when we ask them to conform.

James Dyson

"I am not in business to make money and I am not in business to get big."

James Dyson sighs, leaning back behind the marble-topped table in his vast first-floor corner office at the ever-growing Dyson headquarters in Malmesbury, Wiltshire. It is a warm day in April, the trees are already in leaf in his newly-landscaped car park, their contours reflected across the front of Dyson's coolly modern, wavy-roofed, glass-fronted factory. And just as new life is springing forth, Dyson, the vacuum cleaner king – his factory seemingly under permanent expansion, his research teams

James Dyson

beavering away on top-secret plans for his next coup de theatre, a high-speed washing machine – is pondering the awkwardness of success. The money. The acclaim. The demands made upon you – that was never what he wanted.

So I posit my theory. The key to success is failure. Not other people's failure, but how you respond to your own inevitable failure. Everyone gets knocked back. No-one rises smoothly to the top without hindrance.

The ones who succeed are those who say, right, let's give it another go, who cares what others think? I believe in what I am doing, I will never give up.

Dyson nods. "You're right," he says. "Success is made of 99% failure, you galvanise yourself and you keep going, as a full optimist." But it is not just perseverance that counts, he goes on, it is hope. "I think hope is the most important element in success."

Of course, this mixture doesn't always make you the most personable character in the world. You have to believe when others don't. You have to pursue when others give up. You have to push aside when others get in your way. You have to bounce back when the rest of us would probably say, OK, enough, I'm staying on the canvas.

But look where it has got Dyson. The inventor who for more than a decade was told his idea for a bagless vacuum cleaner was as worthless as carpet dust now sits on a £700m fortune, sees his picture on the cover of *The Sunday Times* Rich List, and finds himself feted by the great and the good and the greedy. All because he never gave up, and in the end broke all the rules by designing, engineering, manufacturing and marketing his own invention. The great British public and others are now happy to pay many hundreds of pounds for one of his finely sculpted machines and even bitter rivals like Hoover have adopted similar technology. And is he content? Mostly, but let's just say that at times he also seems a bit ambivalent about it all.

Contradiction number one, he says, is that he hasn't gone into this to make money and become huge… "But I am in a funny position, in that I *am* making money and I *am* getting big. I am very proud of that, but I wasn't interested in making money. The product is the most important thing."

He smiles, his manner courteous and charming in a rather old-fashioned, aloof sort of way. That is something I wasn't expecting: the sheer upper-crustness of James Dyson. Somehow, after all those stories of him beavering away in his potting shed workshops, I was anticipating something grimier, and something more cerebral. In fact, he is the least likely boffin inventor you could meet. Tall, lithe, exquisitely dressed in dark turtle-neck, blue cotton trousers and black suede loafers, he looks and talks like a big-boned Nigel Havers, only that redoubtable jaw-line giving a hint of the stubbornness underneath. Stubborn, his wife Deidre tells me, is one of the key Dyson adjectives. And, of course, optimistic. "He has always had an absolute belief in what he is doing," she says.

It is that belief which kept him going during the hard times. Anyone still unfamiliar with the story of how he built his business – progressing from the Royal College of Art in the late 60s to designing boats, inventing the ball-barrow and then setting up on his own to produce a revolutionary vacuum cleaner that rival manufacturers tried to kill at birth – should read his autobiography *Against All Odds*. It is remarkable if only for the fact that he names his enemies so plainly, an unusual occurrence in business biographies: people who stood in his way, executives who tried to rip him off, friends and even family who failed to have faith. This is not a man to cross, you realise, reading it. He never forgets.

"Oh God," he laughs when I ask him about it, "the book did cause me a lot of trouble."

Because of the hurt?

No, not really, he says, more because of the names the lawyers made him leave out.

Frightened of another lawsuit?

He laughs again. In some ways the book, like his life, is just a running list of the endless litigation he has been forced to fight here and abroad to protect his invention. Lawsuit after lawsuit after lawsuit.

Doesn't he ever feel he is too litigious?

"Actually, I am not very litigious," he says crisply. "I avoid legal action like the plague, and the only action I have ever started was against someone else who infringed my patent. The rest I defended. But I will fight if necessary and fight hard, and I am *very* competitive."

Born in 1947, the son of a Norfolk public school teacher, Dyson has become a celebrity not just because of the late success of his business – after all, vacuum cleaners can only be interesting for so long, however much money they make you – but because of the manner in which he has chosen to front it. He is not the first design-trained celebrity boss to insist on total control over everything (Sir Terence Conran springs to mind) but he is the first in recent years to have built a manufacturing company of Dyson Appliances' size and to have kept 100% to himself, thus stopping others from challenging his judgement.

Total control comes in all shapes and forms. Dyson preaches openness, honesty, quality, service. If your machine breaks down, you ring a hotline and it is picked up the next day, repaired and couriered back, which if you think about it, is extraordinary. When it comes to corporate strategy, he insists there will be no mergers and acquisitions, no messing with the City. "I could buy companies, tart up their products and put my name on them, but I don't want to do that. That's what our competitors do." There will be no "new brooms", "cutting the fat" or any other business jargon. "It's just not my style. I'm sure we make huge mistakes here, and at times we are too fat, but I think what we are trying to do is worthwhile."

At the same time he runs his factory and offices like an extension of his old garden workshops. He surrounds himself with young staff, many just fresh out of college, and lays down the rules: employees should try to cycle to work, no fry-ups in the canteen, no smoking, no suits and ties…

Cranky?

"I suppose it is," he says, rather languorously, as if he doesn't really care very much what anyone thinks. That kind of placid acceptance of a criticism is very much in character, according to Professor Christopher Frayling, rector at the Royal College af Art, where Dyson sits on the council. "He is always very direct, no bullshit," says Frayling. Some people find that rather intimidating.

He is certainly a mass of irreconcilable contradictions: a brilliant businessman who hates commerce, a champion of the new with some rather old-fashioned values, a skilled inventor who says he would rather be known as "a maker of things".

He says he gets his ambivalent attitude to business from his family – a long line of teachers and vicars. "No-one in my family had anything to do with business," he drawls. "My grandfather, who was a headmaster, wouldn't even speak to a man who moved in next door because he was in trade!"

But you can bet it also comes from having been denied success for so long. When he left the RCA, Dyson worked for his mentor, Jeremy Fry, another engineer-turned-entrepreneur who made a fortune designing and making motorized valve actuators for pipelines. After leaving Fry, it was a long, perilous slog to achieve success, dogged by debt. Even now, Dyson seems to enjoy the position of permanent outsider, not accepted into the manufacturing world because he has so obviously cocked a snook at other industrialists, and not accepted into the design establishment because he manufactures.

He just does his own thing, like the heroes he cites: the Victorian engineer Isambard Kingdom Brunel, the American designer Buckminster Fuller (inventor of the geodesic dome), Mini supremo Sir Alec Issigonis, appliance king Ken Wood. Men of vision who, as he puts it, saw things in a different way. Men who succeeded because, as well as talent and hope, they had resilience.

> *Resilience: the action or an act of rebounding or springing back.*
> *Recoil from something: revolt... The ability to recover readily from or*
> *resist being affected by a setback, illness etc.* (OXFORD ENGLISH DICTIONARY)

Like his vacuum cleaners, he has nothing to hide

Dyson says he has always felt different, ever since his father died when he was a child. "Losing a father makes you feel incredibly disadvantaged emotionally. There isn't that person willing you on, there to help you. No-one there to rebel against or draw things from. You become horribly self-reliant, and you grow up quicker in one sense, and never grow up in another."

Certainly he looks about 15 years younger than his age – he's a health and fitness fanatic, running three times a week and watching what he eats. His son Jacob, also a designer, calls him "Peter Pan" and there is, according to those who have worked with him, a certain childlike quality in his enthusiasms, a naivety which encourages him to break rules and challenge status quos when others might think it batty to do so.

There is also an obsessiveness which often surprises. He is so dogmatic on some issues that at times he seems mildly eccentric. His family tell how he assails smokers in restaurants, lecturing them: "It's just like me farting in your face. How would you like that?" He jumps up and down by the fridge when he sees people spreading butter on toast, going "disgusting, greasy stuff!" And pity the new recruit who turns up in a suit and tie…

"When you see groups of businessmen in suits and ties at hotels and conventions, they do so often look deeply unattractive, don't they?" he says, sounding suddenly foppish, like a character out of an Oscar Wilde play. "They look like a group of policemen or soldiers, rather threatening. We are in a consumer-oriented business and I want everyone here to remember that people are just like us. We are human beings, not businessmen trying to shaft the consumer at home."

Likewise, he thinks an interest in money is rather vulgar, and he is not a fan of paying people bonuses to hit targets.

"I think the whole principle of bonuses is demeaning. If someone needs a bonus to motivate them then they are not the sort of person who should be in business in my view. Somebody is here because they believe in what

I cannot be bothered
what I am doing

we are doing and want to go with that and make a difference and get great satisfaction themselves and achieve things."

Really? Easier to say when you are worth half a billion, I guess. What does he draw as salary?

"I'm not sure I know and I'm not sure I would like to reveal it anyway," he says. (Documents filed in Companies House show he has paid himself millions of pounds since 1996, but then the worldwide turnover of Dyson Appliances – 100% owner: J Dyson – has leapt too, so no-one is complaining.)

What does he spend it all on? A £3m estate bought off Lord Puttnam. Houses in London and France. Constant helicopter and private jet travel. Beautiful furniture for office and new home. If this suggests he has got rather grand, he hasn't really, as everyone from his friends to the local cab-drivers assure me. He bought Puttnam's house because it was only five

convincing other people

is right

minutes from his factory, he uses the helicopter so he can get home quickly when he is away, all he really wants to do is spend time in his beloved engineering department. Time is everything at the moment. "The worst thing for James is not having enough time to fit everything in," says Deidre.

Which is why his obsession for total control will probably have to end soon. No company can grow as fast as Dyson Appliances and refer everything through one man for ever. Nor will Dyson himself be able to attract executives with sufficient experience to manage that growth without offering them a stake in the business. He acknowledges all that, though at the moment he says he is very happy with his young graduates. The only people he ever loses, he says, are those already tarnished with experience of working elsewhere. With his graduates, he is nearly always right.

"I think there are psychological reasons why it is better for me to have 100%, perhaps because I am rather lazy – no, that's the wrong way of putting it – I cannot be bothered with the process of going round convincing other people that what I am doing is right. And you have to do that if you don't control all of it."

But he does agree it is "inequitable" that he should keep 100% in the long term, "because others are making such a big contribution it is right that they should have a stake".

Ah. When?

"There are no plans to do so yet," he says, with a rather winning smile.

Friends point out that he learnt early on in his business life that control is the last thing you give up. He fell out badly with his sister and brother-in-law after they ousted him from the company he had set up to produce the ball-barrow in 1979. Like everyone else, before and since, they presumed that because he was a designer and engineer, he couldn't be trusted to run the business. Dyson was so aggrieved that he didn't speak to either of them for ten years. And now?

"Relations are repaired, but they are not quite what they were before," he says, with his usual disarming honesty. Most people would just say 'fine' but Dyson cannot bear pretence. Like his transparent vacuum cleaners, he really is a man with nothing to hide.

Richard Rogers meets Guy Hands

Resilience is an inner core. Take two completely different men: Richard Rogers, architect, and Guy Hands, financier (in fact, thinking about this, I cannot emphasize *how* different they are – different ages, different outlooks, different achievements, different politics). They have the same disability. Splice together their own accounts of their upbringing. Notice how their parents came from abroad to here, how they were pushed forward with an outsider's perspective, how they coped, how they prospered.

Lord Richard Rogers, architect: "My great-great-grandfather was English, from Sunderland. He went to Venice and stayed. I was born in Florence. Our blood is Italian but there was a snob value in being English in those days – you can find a kinder way of saying it. I was called Richard, not Ricardo, which was very odd, as my father was born in Italy... My father was a physician, a consultant in kidneys. We moved over here because of Mussolini. He worked at St Heliers in south London."

Guy Hands, financier: "I was born in Rhodesia. My mother is a teacher, my father a lawyer. They came here in 1962. I was very young but I think he felt he didn't want to practise law in a country with apartheid. He was a liberal."

Rogers: "My mother was a potter, I was brought up with Bauhaus furniture, modernism was part of my upbringing, medicine and

Richard Rogers

architecture were the two main family areas. I knew I wanted to be an architect at 20. Until then I had no idea what I wanted to do, then suddenly the penny dropped, now I can never think of why. Maybe because my cousin Ernesto Rogers was an architect. I was brought up with Ernesto's works at home. My mother was a great influence. I spoke to my mother every day of my life."

Hands: "We were as poor as church mice when we arrived. I remember the cold of the first winter, when I was three and a half, and I remember being hungry. We used to go to the supermarket on Fridays, and I remember by then I was always starving. For the first three or four years my father was doing solicitor's articles with two then three young children, it was quite a tough situation, articled clerks didn't get paid... What impression did it leave on me? I think it has always made me have a certain sense of the value of money, probably.

Rogers: "I am dyslexic... I had tremendous problems during my education, I was beaten over the head continuously for being stupid. My parents stood by me, but I was sent to all the wrong schools. I went to St John's, Leatherhead, I would have gone to Epsom College if I'd been bright enough, and been a doctor. I don't have happy memories of schooldays. I'm all for education but I don't look back fondly. Till I became an architect I had a tough life."

Hands: "I went to boarding school for two years for my dyslexia. While I was there I developed two interests, one was photography, the other was the school magazine. We charged 1p for it. I think the school was great for my confidence and self esteem, but it did nothing for my academic side. I left school with a spelling age of seven... They let me spend one of my terms there learning Macbeth, I still remember bits of it, another term I did nothing but photos. Another term I spent on the South Sea Bubble and financial disasters, that was very interesting. My parents tried very hard for me to overcome dyslexia academically, and I tried very hard not to work academically."

Guy Hands (right) and Andrew Davidson (left)

Rogers: "Dyslexia affected me because when people say things are impossible I don't believe them. At 16 I was told to join the police and go to South Africa. I think that is because I used to box and they probably thought I could hit the blacks on the head. That was their vision of what dyslexics get to do. Put them in the army or the South African police force."

Hands: Being dyslexic I had a lot of time with my own thoughts, I used to think mainly about political issues. I was very conscious of what was going on in Czechoslovakia. Sounds awful, but I used to watch Open University programmes on religion and philosophy. I was top in maths and physics so I jumped a year and just did sciences, did physics, chemistry and maths for A level. I didn't like it so I switched to economics, maths and physics and lost all interest in science, only wanted to do humanities. In the end I got two A levels, A and E. Think it was E in physics. Other was economics. I had a kidney complaint so I only did two exams in the end. No university would take me for what I wanted to do except Belfast and I didn't want to go there. So I decided I would do Oxbridge entry, did incredibly esoteric logic paper, philosophical reasoning, with questions like, which is better, murder, infanticide or genocide? There were no right or wrong answers, it was just about arguing. I got in."

Rogers: "I got a few O levels after a second try, then went into the army on national service for a couple of years till everyone had forgotten I'd not got exams. Went in a private, came out a private, very difficult to do. Went to Italy and that's where I decided to become an architect. Was it a smooth run after that? Nothing ever is, is it? I often thought I wouldn't work. Because of the dyslexia I had a lot of problems at architectural school, it was not till I was in my final year that I had some kind of understanding of what architecture was about. I had a lot of ups and downs. Even when I started out with Norman Foster at Team 4, I went on Hampstead Heath and cried. I thought I'd never be a bloody architect."

Hands: "Between doing exams and going up to Oxford for my interview I sold encyclopedias. I wanted to make money. Why? I think, um, it was a measure of self-worth, largely low self-esteem, really. I wasn't particularly good at anything so I wanted to find something I could be good at. I'd always had various money-making schemes from the age of 13 onwards, freelance photography, selling pobbles, all sorts of business things. When at school I would literally work 50–60 hours in shops trying to earn money. I think my parents saw it as a phase I would grow out of...

We are not entrepreneurs

Rogers is now one of the world's most famous architects, adviser to governments and commissions, and head of a practice that bears his name, among the most financially successful in Britain. Hands, allegedly the highest-paid man in London's Square Mile, is leaving his job as boss of Nomura Principal Finance, a City heavyweight which, under his guidance, has invested in trains, pubs, army homes and a host of other unrelated items. Hands nearly bought the Dome, which Rogers' practice designed. Neither men see themselves as entrepreneurs. Hands says that he likes rules too much and to be an entrepreneur you must break rules. Both men, however, confound expectations.

The disingenuous dotcom success

"Yeah, I'm into the idea of breaking rules," says Brent Hoberman, founder of lastminute.com. He adds with that goofy Pete Sampras smile: "I'd call myself an entrepreneur."

But surely Hoberman has too many of life's advantages – tall, handsome, charming, rich – to be an entrepreneur? Educated at Eton and Oxford, scion of a South African retailing dynasty, father an investment banker in New York, mother moving from Paris to Portugal via the South of France, sister a successful painter; where's the failure there, where's the resilience?

to be an entrepreneur
break

Then you have to ask yourself: why didn't he just pluck an easy professional job from the tree, as most with his advantages would do?

He says he doesn't think about it, he just does it, relying on luck and optimism. "In every business story there is an element of luck. It's about getting people to back you. I am an eternal optimist and always believed lastminute would work. If you think about all the risks, you never do anything. That's why lots of people have great ideas that they never do." And so he went on to set up one of Britain's best-known online businesses – a site where punters can pick up late bargains on travel, accommodation or entertainment, And where suppliers can find a market for slow-selling (or no-selling) goods.

He is being disingenuous about his motivations, of course. The truth is that, like many entrepreneurs, he was probably a pretty lousy employee. He tried working for other people. Either they rejected him, or took him on

you must

the rules

and regretted it later. After Oxford, he applied to McKinsey, the management consultant. They didn't want to know. Instead he found another consultant, Mars & Co, willing to take him on. They terminated his employment because he spent too much time on his own schemes. So he found another consultant, Spectrum, willing to hire him. Note the jobs: he wanted something where he was telling others what they should do. He left Spectrum to take a job at LineOne, then he put in a stint helping Tim Jackson set up QXL, the online auction business.

(He was reading Jackson's book on Richard Branson at the time. This was his side-subject, the course-work every British wannabe has done over the past two decades: keep up-to-date on Branson, study the tips. "If there was ever anyone who managed a brand incredibly well in the UK," reflects Hoberman, "it was him.")

Brent Hoberman

Rewind: the first time I met Brent Hoberman

He left the room after 30 minutes. He'd just taken a couple of mobile calls, said he had to go and see someone who was in the building. Would I wait? Sure. Back in a mo, says Hoberman, with a curious, nervous laugh of his that goes up a note at the end. And so leaves me alone in the vast first-floor meeting room at his company's Buckingham Gate office in London.

The minutes tick by. The room, I'd say, is about 40ft by 15ft with an enormous conference table running down the centre, 20-odd seats dotted around. I've got time to take in these details. Nineteen awards on the sideboard, a nice picture on the wall, the large catering pot of Nescafé, a kettle. Fifteen minutes go by. Thirty minutes. Oh look, there's a Doris Day CD too. Forty-five minutes. But no CD player. An hour. And no Brent. Or anyone popping in to tell me where he had got to.

Che sera, sera. Had he just forgotten about me? Probably. I never saw him again. After an hour and a bit, I left him a note saying 'had to go', and went home to await his apologies.

Nothing.

So I e-mailed him to say, can we finish the interview on the phone? Sure, he replied, and then almost as an after-thought, sorry I had to dash off. *You're* sorry? I had to waste over an hour of my life looking at a Doris Day CD cover…

That's Brent, laughs one of his friends, before pleading, don't do a hatchet job on him – it's just the way he is. Bit disorganised, always leaping from one thing to the other, but a great visionary and not a nasty bone in his body. "Did he really do that to you?" repeats Martha Lane Fox, lastminute's co-founder. "Oh God, when he does things like that I just want to curl up in a corner and die but really…"

Yes, yes, I know, and he's really charming later on the phone, excited like a schoolboy because he's got lastminute onto 49m chocolate bars in a promotion with Nestlé. "They've sent me cartons and cartons of them," he laughs, "if you want some chocolate, come round." It's very hard to dislike him, even if you've been stood up by him. Yet I was miffed. I hate being rejected.

For Hoberman, being rejected was just part of trying, part of that American "if you're not failing some of the time, you're not trying hard enough" ethos.

Why him?

Hoberman never settled, never dug himself in, instead he plotted and planned, never putting too much faith in anything except that which he

every milestone

you want to

could directly control. I wonder if that was a symptom of his upbringing? Divorced parents, boarding school abroad, always jetting off to see his father on one continent, his mother on another, obsessing about his grandfather, retail magnate Len Shawzin, a fixed spot in a turbulent world.

Hoberman describes his job moves to me as "a logical progression". Much of the time, he admits, he was collecting information, contacts and experience that he needed for his own launch, biding his time, choosing his moment, "always terrified that someone else would do it first". He never faltered, not even when Tim Jackson, keen to keep Hoberman, offered him a chunk of his new company. "He wanted something like £300,000 or £400,000," says Hoberman. "I could have got it, I guess, from family, but I wouldn't have wanted to." He could have turned those hundreds of thousands into many millions once QXL floated, in the heady days of the dot.com boom, but he passed. He has his own plans. He had resilience. You

you achieve,
achieve
more

would just never guess it from meeting him, so young, so casual, so articulate. But then, you haven't done business with him.

Those who have say that beneath the charm, he has huge perseverance. He also doesn't dwell on rejection. Like the relentless womaniser of legend, who takes a 'no' on the chin and moves on, doesn't agonise, doesn't look back, doesn't lose confidence, just keeps on going. When I ask Lane Fox, another former Spectrum consultant, what he was like when they first met, she laughs and says "obsessional, about women and ideas".

That makes him scatty with the everyday, disorganized with the conventional. His friend Rogan Angelini-Hurll describes him as a nightmare in his car, banging a battered VW Golf round London with his mind a million miles away. "Brent is the worst driver in the world," says Angelini-Hurll. "He once told me he couldn't concentrate on driving for more than two minutes at a time and I believe him. Look at the floor by the passenger seat in his car and you'll see the carpet is worn out where the brake pedal should be!" I like that detail. His friends are saying, slow down, concentrate, what are you doing? He's building a multinational at breakneck, bewildering speed.

Only occasionally do you see the resilience slipping, the perseverance confounded by perverse circumstance. First the press loved Brent and Martha. As 1999 moved into 2000, you couldn't move for images of the two, especially Martha, good-looking, sweet-talking, young – symbol for a dotcom revolution that the world wildly over-rated. Then, when sobriety hit the shares and the world woke up with a hangover, the press flipped, and said: awful self-publicists, they deluded us, who do they think they are?

And what had they done?

"You can't manage the press," says Hoberman, looking deadly serious, "you just have to be reactive. People were critical of Martha for getting so much publicity, but it wasn't up to her. Once a few photos are out there with a bit of a story anyone can write about you. So much of what was written was just rehashed with her picture..."

One company that worked with Brent and Martha on their ascendance dubbed them 'Janet and John' because of their naivety.

"...Once I saw us on the cover of the European edition of *Business Week*, I felt then the hype was too high. I said then we are going to get a backlash... recently a friend of mine who is a journalist says that he heard a City editor say 'we are going to get the smug bastards down'.

He has had to wring apologies out of newspapers for factual errors, fight the constant stirring up of envy. "There was one article written by a guy I know, Toby Young, which was the most upsetting article, trying to focus on the envy, when both Martha and I would say we don't experience that around us at all."

Why was it upsetting?

"Because it suggested most people viewed us with envy and... we just don't see that as the case. They are trying to build up an envy that is peculiarly British. Martha and I don't believe we are smug. Someone asked me the other day, how do you stop yourself from being complacent? And I said, you've never met a complacent entrepreneur, it's an oxymoron, every milestone you achieve, you want to achieve more."

But then you don't meet many entrepreneurs who use words like 'oxymoron' either, and maybe that's what has dogged lastminute. Investors, analysts, press: none can really make Hoberman out. Who is this charming, educated, rich kid who has come from nowhere to head one of the hottest companies in Britain? Surely, somewhere along the line, these kids will get swamped? And yet, at the beginning, everyone invested, everyone bought a chunk of the dream, no-one wanted to miss the wave...

Putting the flag in the ground

Resilience is also about resisting temptation. After Hoberman decided to set up lastminute, one of the first meetings he had was with David Landaur, boss of Loot, the sell-anything paper and website. Landaur, says Hoberman, was a friend of his aunt's. "I asked him whether Loot wanted to back the idea, and he was very nice, very helpful, very enthusiastic. And then he said to me, 'why are you showing me all this? Don't do that, keep it secret'. Eventually Loot's approach was 'why not do it as part of us?' but we thought that was not a big enough way to do it. There's no point in putting the flag in the ground and not doing it properly."
Hoberman had a vision, and he stuck to it.

DOUBLE VISION

visionary, optimist ... business as usual

activist,

Waiting for Roddo

London, a warm September night: St James' Church in Piccadilly smells strongly of beeswax and mournful anticipation. It is that kind of church, richly atmospheric, colonnaded, bedecked in finery, as at ease with a religious celebration as a book reading. That morning it had hosted a memorial service for Derek Hill, the artist and confidant of royalty. Hill was also a close friend of my mother-in-law. She doesn't go to memorial services – too depressing – so she sent my wife instead, who reported that the whole congregation stood up obsequiously when Prince Charles entered, which she found rather sad in these democratic times, but that the singing was beautiful.

This evening we stand for no-one. Instead we wait for Anita Roddick, founder of The Body Shop and Britain's most famous female entrepreneur, here to launch her latest book, *Business As Unusual*. The ground floor pews are filling up, there must be 130, maybe 150 people here, couples in suits, women of a certain age with wild hair, a gaggle of gay guys at the back, some blonde Danes, earnest young men carrying bike helmets and bum bags, even some Japanese tourists. I am amazed at Roddick's drawing power. For the past five years I have never found an editor who takes her seriously, let alone one willing to commission an interview with her. They see her as nutty, complicated, over-exposed, beyond the pale. If it was 1650, all the City editors would have burnt her at the stake. Yet so much of what she has espoused and pioneered over the past 15 years – the stakeholder concept, concern for the environment, worries over globalism – has become standard practice for big companies and part of constant government think-tanking. I think her influence has been profound. I would just be wary about telling her.

Waterstone's
Piccadilly

Chain Bookseller of the Year 1999

ANITA RODDICK AT ST JAMES'S CHURCH Business as Usual

Thursday 28 September at 7.00pm

Tickets: £2 redeemable against a purchase of the book

Waterstone's Piccadilly, 203 - 206 Piccadilly, London W1V 9LE
Telephone 0171 851 2400 email: orders@piccadilly.waterstones.co.uk

We are sorry but latecomers will not be admitted to the event once it has started

---

Roddick invite

Tonight, her publishers have done her proud, draping the walls of the church in long banners stamped with huge words VISIONARY, ACTIVIST, OPTIMISTIC that in this context seem, frankly, idolatrous. Then they undermine the effort by misprinting the tickets BUSINESS AS USUAL. Ha! Just another book launch. Sure. But with Roddick, a fizzing firework as likely to blow up in your hand as in the sky, sure is one thing you can never be. Prompt start at 7pm, say the fliers, be there or miss out. Roddick, of course, doesn't get up to speak till 7.15pm. I rather resent the wait, that gap between promise and practice.

And from where I am sitting it is virtually impossible to see her when she stands up. She uses a small lectern next to a 6ft slide screen in front of the altar. A reading light haloes her hair and leaves just her face visible, rectangular and determined, poised over her text. Then she launches into her speech, a tumble of words, rambling and anecdotal, never dull but full of troughs and peaks like an Atlantic swell. You are not quite sure at any time what she is talking about, the problems of ethics, reputation, capitalism, poverty. You swiftly get a sense of the extraordinary drive that has somehow metamorphosized into towering ego, inevitably, as she has reacted to the brick wall of people's attitudes by just boosting herself bigger.

"In the words of my friend Gloria Steinem…" And here are photos of Anita at the World Trade riot in Seattle (guess which side?), and here are photos of Anita in the darkest jungle, and here she's telling us how she gave her book advance to an Indian reservation, and here she's telling us "better naked than Nike" (awkward shuffling of trainered feet among the audience), and here she is saying she is an optimist because she is part-Italian and eats lots of tomatoes.

She is in mid-flow when I leave at 8pm, already late for an incubator drinks bash above a pub in the City. I have a vision of Roddick's head swelling into a giant Stalinist effigy over the altar.

Vision: a) perception or contemplation of an imaginative or spiritual nature; imaginative or mystical insight or foresight. b) ability to plan or form policy in far-sighted way, especially in politics; sound political foresight. (OXFORD ENGLISH DICTIONARY)

Follow behind the elephants and scoop up the dung

The first time I laid eyes on Anita Roddick she was fizzing into a first floor corner office in her pagoda-pastiche headquarters in Littlehampton. Short, sharp, with corkscrew black hair and a surprisingly shy manner, she seemed ill at ease. It was 1996, there were rumours she wanted to buy her company back and take it private, complaints from the City about her attitude, falling profits, a sedentary share price. Her public relations woman sat in – as chaperone, almost – though whether it was to protect Anita from me or Anita from herself wasn't made clear.

Outside it was grey and drab, reflecting the company's fortunes, with January rain falling over the stacked rooftops of the lugubrious Sussex resort. Downstairs, where I'd sat in reception waiting for my audience, you got a greater sense of the vision propelling the enterprise: great wafts of dance music had spilt out of the swing doors from the ground-floor canteen; there were funky sculptures, "Ban Shell" posters, gaggles of young women flocking back and forth. This was the office as vibrant playground, years ahead of its time.

Littlehampton was also Roddick's home, where she was brought up, the daughter of Italian immigrants who ran The Clifton Cafe in the town. She ran a café herself when she was older, the best training possible, she said, for an entrepreneur. It was a view she shared, possibly the only one, with Sir Terence Conran.

The twist in Roddick's background, the really interesting one that she dissects briefly in her 1992 autobiography *Body and Soul*, is the muddle of her parentage. For the first 18 years of her life she was brought up to believe one man was her father, then she found out it was another, her mother's second husband, the man her mother had married after a long affair, the man she thought was only her stepfather. As she tells it, "an enormous weight of guilt had been lifted off my shoulders" when she found out, "because I had never been able to identify with the man I thought was my father; I just didn't like him, didn't like anything about him". And she adored her stepfather. Unfortunately he died of TB aged 39, after only 18 months of marriage to her mum.

And the effect? "A boundless faith in the ideal of romantic love was planted in me forever," wrote Roddick. But also, perhaps, a sense of the possible, that things don't have to be how they seem, that matters can be changed, and that everything is always on the verge of falling apart anyway.

Roddick has been trying to change things ever since, even as she has built up her retail empire into one of the most successful in the UK. As I write this, it has something like 1,700 shops worldwide, over 400 of them company-owned, the rest franchised. Her initial gut instinct that people would buy natural products in reusable bottles with minimal packaging proved to be foresight of the most lucrative kind. Yet few in the business community respect her, few look on her as anything other than a troubled maverick. *The Sun* and *The Mirror* don't revere her like they revere Richard Branson. Is it because she's a woman? Or is it because she is so uneasy with her own success? No-one wants to aspire to something that seems so angst-provoking.

For with success has come the kind of troubled restlessness that eventually just exasperates many who deal with Roddick. Even her most loyal employees have often found her impossible to work with: wilful, angry, illogical, uncompromising, always trying to create a stir. She would take these descriptions as a compliment. Roddick, as a kid, wanted to be an actress. She was offered a place at Guildhall School of Music and Drama. Instead, her mother steered her into teaching, a job she came to loathe. But she never lost her yen for drama. One disgruntled ex-staffer described life with Roddick as like being part of the circus parade – "When you work for Anita your job is to follow behind the elephants and scoop up the dung". Roddick wouldn't mind that opinion either. She can dish it out. Did she

Even her **most** employees *impossible*

really call City folk 'wankers'? Yes, she said when I put it to her, that is an expression I would use...

What was clear that January day was that she was torn. It wasn't as simple as discomfort with her own wealth. I got the impression she enjoyed that – the big house outside Arundel, the other in Scotland, husband Gordon's polo-playing, the constant foreign travel – if only because it gave her clout to change things. No, it was the company itself, her baby, as she liked to describe it. I had caught her on the cusp of her greatest dilemma. Part of her was so desperately proud of what she had created, another part now despised it. "An entrepreneur in a company so big and bureaucratic, it's like death," she said, suddenly very still.

Why?

"Because you are constantly trying to look for creative ways of expressing yourself."

loyal
have often found her
to work with

So set up smaller groups, like Branson.

"We've tried that, but it doesn't foster an entrepreneurial spirit here, it's almost to do with the cosiness of the place, like comfort is a disease. I want to get out and *do* things."

Is that what an entrepreneur does?

"An entrepreneur is someone who wants to shape their own destiny, someone who is always marginalized, always outside, always a bit out of kilter."

She pauses to ruffle that huge snake's nest of hair, then a torrent of words pours forth, the sort of wild flow that turned her detractors' hearts to stone but made a small core of admirers revere her.

"The best dress rehearsal for running any business was running a café which Gordon and I did before Body Shop, during the miners' strike. It was going to be a vegetarian women's place. Within a week we knew we were going to go bust, we had to get a chip fryer and burger machine, had to teach Gordon how to cook; I was out front. And it was the best gathering place in Littlehampton, it was wild, just fabulous, exhausting, working so bloody hard in other people's leisure time; the marriage wouldn't have survived, never saw the kids, mum looked after them. Two years, then I came up with the idea of Body Shop. All I wanted was a controlled life so I could go home at five and be a happily married 30-year-old woman. All working on discontentment, what I didn't want. What don't I have that I want. Want a job where I can close the door and go home. Things I remembered loving were living with tribal groups, which I had always done, and coming up with ideas. There was a time in the 60s and 70s when I used to make my own products, going into Boots, and thinking why can't I buy really small bits of these, like buying one apple. I wanted a shop selling these ingredients; I was using the past as a prologue for ideas, I knew from my travels that you could wash your hair with just about anything. Gordon said it was too bloody sissyish for him and he was going to ride this horse across South America; bloody majestic of him, I got invited to so many parties because of that…"

Iconography with a capital I

Time and again with an entrepreneur like Roddick or Branson – one used to projecting a sense of self onto all their corporate work, whose very iconography is dominated by the capital I – you end up stumbling over the irreconcilable contradictions that define us all. With Roddick, ever-honest, ever-blunt, it is that curious trait of regretting just about every decision she ever made. It was as if she was seeing everything twice: I do this to make the company grow/I do this to make my life shrink.

Why float the company if you hate the financial demands made by the City?

"Because we couldn't get credibility for retail sites. Property owners control retailing – you have to have location – and we weren't being taken seriously… And it's also so sexy, like, why not? It's like when you have this idea, this crazy idea that should never have existed, all you want to do is push it to see how far it can go. There was a huge barometer of reassurance and a way of getting more money, like growing up. I never forget the first day, we went to the Stock Market to see Body Shop float, the big bong of the gong, amazing to see the trading, then they turned round after three hours and said: this is what you are worth. Gordon and I had always measured everything by employees. Suddenly it was money. I remember, we went home in our van and suddenly we thought, crikey, is this how it's going to be, the financial stuff? Quite a road to Damascus; no, we don't want to do this…"

So immediately you had doubts?

"We weren't having doubts, we just knew that we didn't want to be like those giant corporations. It wasn't that we didn't like financial people, but it was like me going on holiday with caravans, or playing darts; I just had no interest in it or their perception of the business."

So you floated for vanity?

"No, when you are in your 40s vanity is not important, not part of my thinking. We were getting excited about getting bigger distribution. That was exciting, getting it round the world, getting little Body Shops in places like Auckland; it was crazy."

You just wanted to be bigger?

"No, I don't think it was size or numbers. You have got to stop thinking in terms of large corporations and get into my head, my little idea, the immigrant kid who had an idea. Well educated in an international way of looking at things, this was my idea, there was only Boots and Estée Lauder and a couple of others, it was cheeky, it was exciting, could it ever be accepted? It was acceptance more than anything."

Because size is a male concern? It was a view she had voiced frequently.

"Absolutely. When men set up a business they set up a small version of a large corporation, whereas women get excited about the idea and how they shape the idea. I don't know too many women in business but it is about doing something remarkable that is more exciting than just the bigness of it. Bigness is very much a male pathology. You can lose your sense of being remarkable by being big."

Yet you are big.

"No, Body Shop is not seen as a big company internally, it's seen as a multilocal company. The relationships we have are with our head franchisees, and they're quite remarkable."

But should an entrepreneur ever run a public company? When I ask her if she should take the company private again, she says: why should I want to stay public is a better question.

"The company is so much built on dimensions other than profit motives that the notion of the braveness of the ideal of what we want to achieve can only be protected if we have a thumbprint on it. This is about stewardship. What happens to the most remarkable people in this company if I go? Who wants another bloody faceless cosmetics company?

So set up a succession? It's what anyone else would do…

"It doesn't work like that. The minute profits go down it isn't seen to be doing as well, because we have a society that only wants short-term profits and gets into a maelstrom of fear and innuendo. You can't hold onto the braveness. To work 20 years in this company and then end up an Estée Lauder, I would pack up and go today."

What is she so uncomfortable about? The demands of shareholders?

Look, she says, this does not mean, as some have interpreted, that she thinks the financial figures are unimportant. "I am not a dickhead. Of course I want to know what the figures are. But to concentrate only on the figures and the interests of shareholders is dumb. 'When you think about it, to have such a small layer of interest take up so much of a company's measurement is bizarre. If a shareholder puts £2,000 into a company why should the notion of a shareholder have more rights than the notion of an employee or the community or the environment? It's a bizarre philosophy which I am not part of at all."

She remembers the sort of strange, ignorant questions she got when she met major investors. "Are we a husband and wife team? Do we want to do franchising? If they were putting millions into us they should have known we were a franchising organization. Never had much respect for financial reporters either. Mostly they don't know how to add up and mostly they don't know how to write… It's great when they ask about the culture or the products, but the analysts, well, I've never known an analyst ask about a product."

Does she think there is a feminine as opposed to a masculine style of business?

"I don't think we have it here but that has changed over the last few years. We brought in a management consultant who was so hierarchical; we brought him in because we never had any sort of strategy or marketing department, we knew the first name of everybody and their grandmother's but couldn't give them a job description; just come in and see what happens, as cavalier as that. Didn't have a five-year plan or a two-year plan. It was really how do you survive this speed of growth? We had to deal with the recession very fast; we didn't know how to deal with America. We had a yearning in the company, almost a heart-sickness, for more structure. People wanted job descriptions and measurements, so we

the behaviour who *are successful,* *they imitate*

brought in this management consultant, I don't even want to name him because I dislike him so much.

"No, it was a catalyst for understanding where some of the dilemmas were and opening discussions. Look, this is death for me, where I start hyperventilating. Women like a flatter structure. I am more comfortable with a management level than a board level, I have never been appropriately confident to function at board level. I think women are more collaborative, more inclusive, they do not intrinsically like hierarchies, they talk feelings to each other. Immediately you put a structure in, you get people saying, how do I get onto the board? It's about the style of communication. Women do best in informal networks, in circular areas. Where we have lost it at this time is we have lost the role of importance of women in this company. Women's work is often unremarked upon and often invisible. You see them give away power all the time, they do not like confrontation. And the behaviour patterns of women who are successful, that's sad, they imitate male behaviour."

patterns of women that's sad,
male behaviour

Is it a hopeless situation?

"No, I just think feminine qualities have to be more appreciated."

Do female journalists understand what she is doing?

"Female journalists do not support women. Bel Mooney is a classic example. Formulaic silliness. Why fucking read it? It's a formula for writing. It's about an agenda for how to get an article printed. There's such a poverty of praise in this country, people cannot praise without either being seen as obsequious or whatever…"

Why we love Anita Roddick really

Roddick never took the company private, of course. The tussle continued, year after year, with her vision of what the company should be, blurring the alternative vision articulated by an increasingly mainstream management. I'm not quite sure how or if she resolved the dilemma.

I don't think anyone is. By the end of the 90s she was semi-detached, "president" of The Body Shop, free to write and campaign and lecture, with her own office away from Littlehampton. Presumably executive involvement in the company was discouraged.

In 2000, shortly after I saw her in London, she caused a stir when she told the Cheltenham Literary Festival that anti-ageing creams didn't work. The press attempted to whip it up – Roddick slags off her own industry shock horror – but it fizzled out. Where had they been for last 15 years? This wasn't another Gerald Ratner, calling his own products crap, just the same old, unconventional Roddick, telling people what they knew anyway, but preferred to forget when they bought into the dream. Then there was her support for the anti-globalism movement. She sent letters to newspapers saying that she had never condoned terrorism or violent action in support of her causes. Well, maybe I wasn't concentrating at your book launch, Anita, but it seemed to me you rather revelled in the Seattle riot events. But you're right, I am being unfair, there was no support for violence.

Before I left that January day, with Littlehampton looking as grey and uninviting as a worn-out raincoat, she told me of her latest vision, a New Business Academy. "I want to think about management in the future, there are too many issues that are not being discussed: human rights in business, gender perspectives, spiritual perspectives." She had got the seed money together for it, was looking for a location, wanted it to be residential. She saw it as an adjunct to an MBA, doing masters in socially responsible business, environmental management and sustainability. She thought the Shells and BPs of this world would be "adoring to come".

"Why don't you come?" she said to me. "You interview business people. You can't just be a barometer all the time. How about being someone who can help fashion a new way of thinking? There are so many fantastic ideas not given airspace just because Fortune 500 companies aren't using them or whatever."

> For double the vision my eyes do see
>
> And a double vision is always with me.
> **William Blake**

She'd got me.

Eventually I said, oh, you know, I like being freelance, and who'd pay for me to do the course?

"Well," she said, "you could be a reporter on *Eco-Management*."

Could I? Does it exist? I'll think about it, I replied.

When I said goodbye she pressed her autobiography into my hand. In it, she wrote, "To Andrew, life is no more complicated than loos and work!" Indeed.

Yo! Sushi

For some entrepreneurs, vision is their greatest asset and their biggest flaw. Their vision is so powerful, so all-encompassing, that they can barely see anything else, certainly not the minutiae required to run a company. They can think it up, they can foresee it, but they don't want to do it. Does Roddick really want to run The Body Shop as a gargantuan, multinational entity? No, of course not. But what of the people left behind? Someone has to clear up after the entrepreneur, to ring-fence the project and allow it to grow with stability. They plot to redirect the entrepreneur's focus, to release them from mundanity, to allow them to concentrate on creativity. Think of the tension.

Simon Woodroffe came late to building a business empire. Public school drop-out, one-time roadie, former lighting engineer and set designer for rock shows, occasional media salesman and ski bum, he'd done a lot of things before setting up Yo! Sushi, but building a restaurant chain wasn't one of them. At 48, he had spent half his life creating, succeeding, failing, much like the rest of us. In his early 40s, he had decided this was his last chance, his one opportunity to really make it, and he worked hard for it. He plotted, he planned, he steamrollered his way into the public consciousness with his concept: a conveyor belt sushi bar where plates trundled past customers, and they picked off what they wanted. Already popular in Japan, he gave it a contemporary twist: hi-tech surroundings, a Californian ambience, a funky name. Yo! Sushi.

He opened his first restaurant in 1997 to huge acclaim, a handful more in London followed. Woodroffe was everywhere, giving interviews about this, public lectures about that. Publicity was his sword and he put his rivals to flight. And then it went eerily quiet.

Not just gimcrack

The problem you've got, I tell Woodroffe rather presumptiously, is that you arrived with a bang, and everyone expected you to roll out your idea everywhere, and then, what happened? It just seemed to stall.

Woodroffe nods, smiling faintly. Outside the February light is fading, 2001 just staggering into muddy existence. He's sitting in an unkempt glass and concrete booth – his office, I think – off London's Clerkenwell Road. His denim shirt lolls open. His desk is piled with papers; letters and press cut-outs decorate the walls. All rather haphazard, unlike the scrupulously cut blond sideburns that trace his solid jaw-line.

No, he says cautiously, we didn't roll out the Yo! Sushi concept as fast as everyone thought because we had a "confidence thing".

Meaning?

"Oh, we were talking to so many people about franchising and joint ventures," says Woodroffe, in his classless, musicbiz drawl, "and we opened in Bluewater in Kent and that didn't do as well as we thought; it was a different crowd and we had it in the wrong place."

So Woodroffe, who'd just won an Emerging Entrepreneur of the Year award – remember, nothing threatens a business like one of those – backed off, rethought, rehired, and is only now, four years after launch, returning to the growth trail. His groovy, wood and steel restaurants, complete with trademark conveyor belts, are once again appearing in new sites across London.

Yo! Sushi was opening in Edinburgh, with two more in Scotland following. Ten outlets will become 20 by the end of 2002. A deal in America is in the offing, too. Oh, and Woodroffe has written a short tome, *The Book of Yo*, about what he's learnt as a successful emerging entrepreneur.

Bit of a hostage to fortune, that, so early in the business's lifespan?

"No," he says, "there is a lot of interest in being an entrepreneur nowadays. For me, it's been such a big growing thing; if it all went wrong, I could earn a living just *talking* about how it all went wrong." He grins his handsomely toothy smile, blue-grey eyes sparkling, before adding hastily, "but I am

Simon Woodroffe

fairly confident now that I will be OK for the rest of my life, whatever happens."

He's probably right, for Woodroffe, if nothing else, has tapped a rich vein in the country's need to hear more about business. He speaks at conferences, he pushes himself around, he makes himself available – all part of his longer-term plan to put a face to the Yo! brand, move it on from restaurants into related areas. It's the same scheme, he says, as that perfected by his role models. Who they? Richard Branson, of course, and Stelios. Woodroffe's quite open about that, quite unashamed about his copycat techniques, quite happy to invite your criticisms.

Which is good, because what you want to say is, excuse me, all you've done is open a clutch of gimmicky restaurants, how can you sound off like you've created an empire? It's too calculating, people won't be fooled. They'll turn.

He shrugs. "Maybe it will happen to me but if I try to stop that happening then I am not being true to myself, I am being insincere, aren't I? I like being listened to, it goes back to being a child…"

And there is something rather winning about Woodroffe's honesty, and his part-naive/part-calculating approach. Similarly, his book, a loose mix of personal reminiscence, old saws and pertinent quotes – barely 5,000 words by my count – is surprisingly readable, and his faddish restaurants and bars are not all gimcrack either. Others who know more about the market than me have avowed as much. Luke Johnson's Belgo group opened talks to buy the chain 18 months ago (they didn't offer enough, says Woodroffe). Julian Metcalfe's Pret A Manger outfit is rolling out a rival concept, Itsu.

Most acknowledge that, when the systems are working properly, Woodroffe's idea is a winner and the man himself is an original, who could, in tandem with others, have the same effect on British eating habits as the Pizza Express founder Peter Boizot. Thirty years ago, how many pizzas did you see in supermarkets? Now look at the shelves. And sushi is already huge in America, and creeping into supermarkets here.

"What's interesting is that sushi has been around for a while but Simon's given a real turbo-charge to its identity," says Ian Neill, chief executive of the rival Wagamamma chain, "and he's added value with all the bells and whistles."

Those "bells and whistles" include drinks-dispensing robots that swear when you impede them, beer-pumps at tables, all manner of hi-techery to keep the outlets' young clientele stimulated and amused. It means a lot can go wrong – one reviewer witnessed the conveyor belt seize up while plates crashed to the floor – but it also gives each venue the feel of an event.

There are other plus-points. While the robotics appeal to the boys, the low-calorie food wins it a wide female audience too. The restaurants, at an average £450,000 a pop, are also relatively cheap to fit out and, needing less service staff, highly profitable to run. "The most profitable restaurants per square foot that I have ever worked with," says Robin Rowland, Yo! Sushi's managing director, who should know, as his CV includes Whitbread, Grand Met, Scottish & Newcastle and City Centre Restaurants (Est Est Est, Caffe Uno, Wokwok, Garfunkel's and more). In short, Woodroffe's got all ends covered.

The only problem is managing the growth – or as his team intimate, managing the entrepreneur himself. At one stage Woodroffe wanted to build the restaurant chain and expand the brand on his own. His vision was clearly bigger than just eating out; he had wizard plans for Yo! hotels, Body Yo! health spas, Yo! nightclubs, all of which made his bankers – he was backed by NatWest, now it's Barclays – rather nervous. It was also unrealistic, because the UK's eating out-scene, a dangerous jungle at the best of times with elephants like Bass and Whitbread stomping around, is not for inexperienced enthusiasts.

And that, as Woodroffe admits, is exactly what he is. Ex-roadie, lighting engineer, set designer, mediaman… Hence the decision to hire in people like Rowland, and catch his breath before pushing on.

In other words, Woodroffe had reached the point where it gets really interesting. The history of innovative restaurant chains such as Pizza Express is one of quirky creatives doing the vision thing before handing over to others who put in the systems and manage the efficient expansion. Cue exit of founder. Woodroffe owns 85% of Yo! Sushi but is expected to sell off a chunk of his shares eventually. Will he be able to hang onto control once the systems men take over?

And it is an open secret that, like many creative people, Woodroffe is not the easiest boss to work with. Moody, short attention span, fast-moving focus. "It's like surfing," says one of his managers. "You've got to ride his wave of consciousness each day… He's very driven but he also has a foul temper." Certainly while Woodroffe seems confident on top, you can tell he's rather more anxious beneath, keener for reassurance and acknowledgement, like a salesman who's not fully convinced by his own product. Whether the product in question is himself or his restaurant operation is a moot point.

Attention! to detail

Woodroffe says he gets the worry from his dad, a former army officer – Brigadier Woodroffe, late president of the Indian Cavalry Association – who was "a very charming man, but underneath it all a very anxious guy".

Part of that anxiety, no doubt, was fuelled by Woodroffe and his younger brother Patrick getting heaved out of Marlborough in their early teens. He was never particularly happy there, teased because he had been to an even posher prep school. "They called me Lord Snooty," he shrugs, even though his parents were actually fairly impoverished. The problems at school, he

Success has before I was

adds, contributed to his parents' divorce and his subsequent "slight estrangement" from his father.

But a lot of the anxiety just stemmed from his dad's constant worry about appearance. "We were brought up to make the right impression, to always do the right thing; if you don't manipulate the world to see things how you see things, then everything will go wrong."

Some of that, you would guess, has rubbed off on Woodroffe himself, who likes to make a bit of a show himself with his yellow suede shoes and Gap denim demeanour, and his new-found love of public speaking. But the inherited anxiety, he says, also underpins his business style. "It's what breeds in me a real attention to detail, always thinking ahead, always taking problems out of the pocket, blowing them up bigger and dealing with them early on. We all actually know in a sense what will happen to us, if we have the courage to look inside, to take the problems out and look at them and deal with them…"

hanged me,
bitter and
resentful

He cites his experience of therapy as another key to his impetus. It helps you manage people, he says. "It's about understanding what all the people who are working for you feel. I call it x-ray specs. One of the great expressions that I've heard is 'the stuff that you don't know you don't know'. I am very open like that. I use all that stuff all the time."

He says he's tried Jungian analysis, group therapy – for wheening himself off tobacco – been on "five or six" personal development courses. He's also "done all the drugs" in his rock'n roll years, been married (for a year), got a daughter, barely had a girlfriend in eleven years since he got divorced, and is quite happy to chat about all that.

"Well, er, one girlfriend, actually, since I was married. It hasn't happened, I'm very happy living on my own, I'm not out there looking…" Now, he says, he keeps a country home in the same Rutland village as his ex-wife. They're good friends, their daughter pops between the two. "I suspect the villagers think it's very strange."

But, he says, he has rarely been happier. "Success has changed me," he adds, typically blunt, "I'm just a nicer person. Before I was bitter and resentful." That, he says, was because he had tasted failure, and he was always conscious of how his younger brother Patrick seemed happier and better grounded. Sibling rivalry? You bet. Patrick Woodroffe, 46, a successful lighting designer (clients: the Rolling Stones, Bob Dylan and one Millennium Dome), says that, though they get on well now, his big brother probably feels he's had a rougher ride, with some justification. More pressure from their father, a harder time at school – "school was shit, really" – a bad patch in the 80s when his marriage collapsed.

Yet through it all, he was constantly protective of Patrick. He helped him get started in the rock world, and then watched in surprise as his gregarious younger brother built a thriving business. "I think he probably feels he never got the gratitude he deserves," says Patrick. Simon, after designing stage sets for stars such as Rod Stewart and the Moody Blues and for industrial shows, chucked the whole thing in. Why?

"I had a couple of bad experiences and in a short period of time lost my confidence."

Confidence, masking that anxiety, is clearly a key to Woodroffe. He only regained it, he says, when a friend gave him a job selling television rights for rock concert footage. He was good at that, spent eight years at it, earning great money, transforming himself from a 70s hippy into an 80s shark, slicking his hair back, smoking cigars. "Yeah, I was playing the role of making money," he says, "but I was never happy, though I was a good salesman."

Eventually he chucked that in, too, succumbed to divorce and later a midlife crisis. He moved to the Swiss Alps, living off income from some deals he had cut, skiing, climbing, hanging out with the other "ski bums". Then the money ran out, so he came home determined to give business one last try. "I had to support the family and myself, there was not much capital left, I was employable but I didn't want to do that. I thought, here I am, this is it." And so he remodelled himself yet again, this time as a 90s entrepreneur.

He plotted the options meticulously, with notes written in old exercise books, now up on his office shelf. "I am an obsessive notetaker," he says, "and I started writing down all the ideas I had for a business, and what I thought about things. What I realized workwise was that I wanted to get away from being a middle-man and be at the sharp end, be a front person, like a retailer. So I decided I wanted to retail something, and started researching a whole number of things, to see what came up trumps."

Sandwich bars, indoor rock-climbing, sports marketing. He was never sure about restaurants. "I always thought that restaurants were for failures, for people who couldn't do anything else."

Eventually a Japanese friend nudged his thinking. "He said, 'what you should do is a conveyor belt sushi bar staffed by girls in black PVC miniskirts!' And I had never heard those words, conveyor belt sushi bar. I just thought, God, how much will it cost to ring up Japan to find out about that?"

But then things kept falling into place. He went through the trade department of the Japanese embassy in London, and started getting material sent to him from interested suppliers, including full instructions, in English, on how to set up a conveyor belt sushi bar (from a manufacturer who sold the belts).

And Woodroffe walked and talked his way round the restaurants of London. "It's unbelievable how much people want to help you if you ask. When I started I knew nothing, but I walked into a Japanese restaurant in the Fulham Road, told the guy there what I wanted to do, and you cannot believe how much he told me, he told me everything!"

He got the timing right. Sushi was taking off here; it was already big in America. Yet professional restaurateurs outside the Japanese community were reluctant to buy into it. "I kept asking, why hasn't someone else done it if it's such a good idea, but professional restauranteurs wouldn't touch it, it's very complicated dealing with raw fish."

He got the publicity right. He certainly wasn't the first to open a conveyor belt sushi bar in London, but he was definitely the loudest (leading Pret's Metcalfe to sniff that Yo! was "marketing-driven" whereas his Itsu chain was more focused "on ingredients").

And he was probably the cheekiest. When another rival opened before Woodroffe at Liverpool St station (with the same concept – customers pick what they want off the display, pay by the plate) he spent hours there, posing as a customer, sussing out its weaknesses, refining his own idea.

"It was the best thing that could have happened," he says, "because I could watch, and study, and see where they went wrong."

Woodroffe went in with tape-measures, looking under tables, studying the works; all very discreet, of course, the owners never knew. He even took his bank manager in to firm up the finance. "They did the bar in a very Japanese way, I wanted ours to be very modern and hi-tech, very Californian."

In all it took him two years to get the money, the site and the people together to open the first Yo! Sushi. It was shiney and new and attracted big publicity, though he still had doubts. "First I had the voice saying it's not going to work, then I had the voice saying it's going to be very successful… and within a few weeks the numbers were going up and up and up, it was like having a hit record."

Certainly, he wasn't the only one having doubts. His own brother, who helped design the lights for Yo! Sushi, backed off when asked to take a stake. He just wasn't convinced it was worth the investment, even though he'd given his time. "Simon hated restaurants, and the people who ate in them. I just couldn't give it to him," says Patrick.

Yet he got it right and everything went fine until the Bluewater branch opened and success stalled. Why? Wrong place, wrong people, he got over-confident – Woodroffe can reel off the reasons. Crucially, he was distracted by all the offers coming in from overseas for licensing the Yo! Sushi concept.

As one of his advisers puts it, he forgot ground-rule-one for establishing a chain: "When you've got four or five restaurants, they have all got to work properly. And number five, and number six, and seven and eight as well. It's only when you have got twenty or more that you can afford to have one underperforming... The thing that is great about Simon is that he recognized he is not a restaurateur." And he did something about it.

"Yeah, it was a people thing," shrugs Woodroffe. "I had a hit restaurant started with a bunch of amateurs led by me. I mean, I hired a good restaurant manager and good chef but I'd never run a restaurant. In previous businesses I'd been called a steamroller because when I do something, I really want it to be perfect, when I see something is not right, if I don't fix it right now, in my head I think the whole thing is going to fall apart. Why can't others see it! So I'm not very tactful. The big thing I have learnt is to let go and let others..."

So he's taken a back seat to concentrate on design and publicity, and is now allowing others to get on with running the day-to-day business. He can give more time now to "new concepts".

Everybody happy?

No, because it is Woodroffe's love of new concepts and creativity that frightens those outside, and inside, the Yo! team. A few of the *concepts* produced so far, such as making sushi for supermarkets and offering catering and home delivery, have proved adroit in expanding the market.

Others – the possibility of opening Yo! hotels, for example – appear ambitious and very, very expensive. Woodroffe also seems, as the chairman of another restaurant group delicately puts it, increasingly caught up in his own legend.

Certainly he spends a lot of time talking about himself and his plans – a deliberate policy, because he believes that talking about things makes them happen. But that only increases the pressure on his team. "It looks like we'll do America," he tells me. "I came back from America yesterday, we're going to partner one of the big American companies."

Did he really say that? asks one close to him when I query it. "The thing is, we can't stop him, that's what people like Simon are like, they have got to have dreams, got to be ambitious… He may be forced to eat a huge amount of humble pie eventually, but we make sure he doesn't destroy what he has already created."

So already, what he has created is being delicately prised from him. Like many visionary entrepreneurs, Woodroffe faces the toughest conundrum: the bigger his business becomes, the less suited it may be to his talents. Few could imagine him as the boss of a large organization. "Going through the tedium of all those tasks, bringing people along, checking this, checking that," says one, "I don't think so…"

But he is brilliant at vision. "I've got this idea," says Woodroffe, "for the Yo! Sushi in the City, to do different prices at different times of the day, depending on what everyone else is buying." So if demand is high, prices go up. If the restaurant is empty, prices go down. "I've got to get it right," he says, "but it could be real fun. And if a restaurant is empty in the middle of the afternoon it *should* be cheaper." And you think, yes, he's right, why didn't *I* think of that.

He really believes he can take the Yo! spirit – he sums it up as wacky, fun, fearless – into other arenas. "Because we are not rich bastards who cynically conceived a brand, it sort of grew and we have a lot of people supporting us now. I drive one of the little Yo! Mercs" – the company car, little A class runarounds with a large Yo! on the side – "and a lot of people shout Yo! at me, it's all good fun, there's strength in all that."

He continues: "I think it's right for its time, it could be lots of things. Look, I'm exaggerating to make a point, but it could be perceived in the same breath as Virgin or EasyJet. If you look round the world, no-one else apart from Branson and Stelios has had that kind of idea. Well, John Lennon said, 'life is what happens to you while you're busy making other plans', but it could go anywhere..."

And Woodroffe, you guess, could natter all day. Like any boy who was teased at school and outstripped by his brother, he just wants a little popularity, a little acknowledgement. The extraordinary thing is, despite the look-at-me! tendancies, even his rivals quite admire him. Don't beat up on him, says one, "like all positive guys, Simon adds a little sparkle to everything, everything's an opportunity".

But will he still be running Yo! Sushi in five, ten years' time? Will he want to? Or will he, like Roddick, find a bigger cause, a better purpose?

I want him to be safe

While I am talking to Simon Woodroffe's brother Patrick on the phone, he makes an interesting comparison. He's friends with James Dyson, he says, and you know what Dyson and Simon Woodroffe have in common? Single-mindedness. Whatever anyone else thinks, they are convinced that theirs is the right way to do something, and they push it through. They see what others don't and never lose that vision, always stay resilient, never get deflected by the carpers and non-believers. That doesn't make them easy people to be with, but it has defined their success. The really great entrepreneurs have to have that combination: vision and single-mindedness. Without one, the other has no purpose, and no fulfilment.

Then Patrick asks, with genuine concern, what do you think Simon will do with Yo! Sushi?

I don't know, I reply.

"Oh, well, I'm desperate for him to sell," says Patrick. "I just want him to be safe."

Slowly, cautiously

There is another way, of course, as exemplified by the visionaries who are so quiet they can barely be heard by you and me. They are not the icons, the rule-breakers, the self-promoters who encapsulate the consumer proposition in their very essence. They are the ones who, by dint of personality or quirk of strategy, travel softly through the corridors of

He is a careful man,
making

power, persuading only those they need to persuade, avoiding the spotlight. If you asked them, they would deny being entrepreneurs at all – to claim the tag would be a shout on a still night. They work more effectively without it.

Tea at the Savoy with Sir Michael Bishop

Sir Michael Bishop spent the 90s looking out from behind wide, plastic-rimmed, bi-focal glasses. They shrink his dark eyes slightly, making them even more difficult to read. Bishop has spent over 20 years building up British Midland into the UK's third-biggest scheduled airline (after British Airways and Virgin Atlantic). He has done it quietly, without ostentation, playing a smartly diplomatic game by rarely taking sides as BA and Virgin slugged it out. Since he led the management buy-out of British Midland in 1978, he has made the company his own, shrewdly selling off stakes here and there, to SAS, to Lufthansa, when it needed the links or the money, while retaining a sizeable chunk of control for himself.

who doesn't like
enemies

He has thought about taking the company public but has never done so. That, I suspect, would dent his power. Many in the airline business have enormous admiration for the way he has slowly, cautiously built his business while others – Freddie Laker, Harry Goodman – have shot off and burnt out. Lord King, former chairman of BA, once described Bishop as "a quiet little operator". Some might take that as dismissive, but to Bishop it's an accolade. He has always had a vision of exactly what he wanted to achieve: security. "You have to remember this business is a cyclical beast, either famine or feast," he says. "I have never wanted to get into the position where you get caught by the downturn."

He is a neat, courteous, plump man, still, when we met, the young side of 60, with a round face, a balding pate, cropped silver hair and a broad white moustache clipped to within a centimetre of his top lip. That precision is reflected in his dress sense too: pinstripe suits and silk ties. He is dapper without seeming overly well-dressed.

Sartorial elegance aside, he is a difficult man to pin down in interview. There is an edge of wariness to him. You can see it in the press photos, as if he is frightened of the world looking in at him. He keeps his private life very much to himself, and when discussing anything, he is so remorselessly polite and even-tempered that it is often hard to gauge his true opinions. Above all, according to colleagues, he is a careful man, who doesn't like making enemies, but is not averse to taking a few risks occasionally, if the business benefits are great enough.

He invites me to the Savoy Hotel. He is a dedicated Savoy fan, taking a suite two or three days each week, conducting his London business there as if setting up a proper base away from his Midlands head office is really too time-consuming. Generally the hotel gives him the same rooms on the sixth floor facing off-street. The rooms – sitting room, bedroom, bathroom – are small, the view is grim, all steamy pipes and grimy roof, but the nights are quiet and it is, he says, opening the door, a fine place to do business from. As Bishop is a man with a personal worth of, at the last count, close to £200m, running a business with a turnover nearing £1bn, you can't help feeling that he could have booked something grander, even at (especially at) the Savoy.

He strips off his jacket and plonks himself down on a floral sofa under a print of Wallingford Castle in his rather bland sitting room. He apologizes for keeping me waiting. He'd been buying planes. Of course. What do I want to know? he asks, speaking softly, in an accentless, gruff tone so quiet that sometimes I can barely hear him. Well, I reply, the usual things: what makes him tick, why he is good at what he does, what has enabled him to build up such a successful business against the might of rivals like BA. His eyes give nothing away. There's not even a raised eyebrow. He could be lost in thought about his jet deals, or the bowl of fruit on the side table.

It can't be shyness, as Bishop is not slow to put himself about when the cause demands it. He has, in his time, been chairman of Channel 4, where he is credited with saving the company from privatization, and is well known in some circles as chief cheerleader (and funder) for the D'Oyly Carte theatre group, the Gilbert & Sullivan specialists who spent much of the past decade fighting hard for Arts Council money. To others, of course, he is still best remembered as the man clearly devastated when a BM plane went down at Kegworth in the East Midlands in 1989 in one of Britain's worst air disasters. It is not too much of an exaggeration to say that the Kegworth crash, and the dignified, sensitive way in which he and his company handled the catastrophe, catapulted Bishop into public life. Bishop admits as much privately, though obviously it is awkward for him to acknowledge that he personally benefited from it.

Let's talk about his childhood and family, I suggest.

"My grandfather was born in Wellington, New Zealand, my father was born in Melbourne, Australia. He fought in the First World War, serving in the Dardanelles and in Belgium. He was deafened by shelling and went to military hospital in Wiltshire. He married here in the 1920s, then married again in the 1930s to my mother."

Is he like his father?

Bishop mulls this over. He shares his father's love of Australia, he says – he goes there every year – and if he has inherited any characteristics, it is probably his father's singlemindedness and determination. Despite his disability, his father built up a successful small business in Cheshire customizing commercial vehicles. His mother also worked, as a mannequin, modelling clothes for shoppers at major department stores.

It was, says Bishop, a very close family. His father's deafness made him an intensely private man, with little social life. Bishop himself was sent away to school at nine. "I think my parents anticipated rather wisely that it would be good for me as an only child." He never performed well at school, excelling only in his ability to get "could-do-better" reports. But he had one advantage over his peers: he knew exactly what he wanted to do. He had been obsessed with aviation since he was a boy. Holiday jobs working for an aerial photography business at Manchester airport, near where he was brought up, confirmed the passion. "I never had any periods of doubt where I drifted around. I never thought of university. I always knew what I wanted."

Does he regret it now, missing university?

Bishop looks thoughtful for a moment. "I think I might have known more if I had read economics or law at university." Then he breaks into a grin. "Certainly I could avoid spending lots of money now on people who know about those things!"

Like many very rich, self-made men, Bishop has the kind of business brain that watches the pennies closely. He may run a Rolls-Royce and a private plane, keep two large homes (in Edgbaston and Leicestershire), and command his own set of rooms at one of the world's most famous hotels, but he doesn't like to be thought of as extravagant. Hence perhaps the modest nature of his Savoy rooms.

Does it cost a lot to run a suite at the Savoy?

Oh, he couldn't possibly tell me that, he says, with a little smile. Tens of thousands of pounds a year? He just looks at me. Does he get a discount? Ha! he guffaws, then changes the subject.

Why him?

There are lots of reasons, says Bishop, why he has been successful where others haven't. Luck has played a part. At the tender age of 21, working at Manchester airport in the early 1960s, he had set up his own aircraft handling business for a locally based airline. When that was taken over by British Midland Airways, a small company operating out of East Midlands airport, he joined the new outfit. Right company, right time. By 1969 he was general manager; by 1972, at the age of 30, he was managing director. BM was running charter services to Barcelona and Basle and developing scheduled routes too. He had a good team around him, in particular two partners who eventually joined him in buying out the company: Stuart Balmforth, who handled the finance side, and John Wolfe, who headed engineering. Bishop plotted company strategy – which routes, what services, where to get the planes – with quiet shrewdness. He always had the vision of how to survive in the toughest of markets.

It was his talent for sourcing planes that led to Bishop's smartest deal, the management buy-out he led in 1978. He borrowed the money to do the deal from an enormously rich dentist in California who had invested his wealth in two Boeing 707s. Bishop, sniffing for cheap planes, agreed to lease the 707s in return for a £2.5m loan to buy out BM. The dentist got 25% of the company, and later sold out. Bishop and his managers got 75%, and are now very rich indeed.

shareholder's demands

can only

But they have worked hard for it. Bishop's second shrewdest move was to sense the change in political mood in the early 80s, when he lobbied hard for the right to fly from Heathrow on domestic routes head-to-head with BA. Not surprisingly, BA lobbied just as hard against him getting the slots, but Bishop persevered and won. BM had in fact been flying from Heathrow since 1969, another smart Bishop decision, but the licence for the Heathrow to Glasgow route in 1982 was followed by services to Edinburgh and Belfast. The Heathrow slots have, in some rivals' opinions, been BM's greatest bit of good fortune, protecting Bishop from anything BA could throw at him, but it took real determination to make a go of them. "The London-Belfast service was a financial disaster for the first couple of years. Anyone else would have chucked it in," remembers one colleague. "But Michael is very courageous, he takes the right risks." And the risks pay off. From 1984 to 1998, passenger loads on the London-Belfast route doubled from 500,000 per year to over a million.

for short-term profits
undermine
long-term strategy

Bishop then took the fight for liberalization overseas. By the 90s he had established BM as Heathrow's second largest operator, offering "value for money" business travel. It was also the only privately run airline to challenge national flag-carriers on the main European routes. "This business is unique and special," one of Bishop's senior executives told me. "I think even the regulators appreciate that." By then Bishop was letting his managers run the shop, while he concentrated on the bigger picture: politics, regulation, competition. Slow but sure was the key motto. Others have described Bishop's progress as like the tortoise against the hare. He never looked like winning, but he did.

And part of sticking to the vision, the double vision that no-one else could quite see, was avoiding the obvious moves. He resolutely kept the main business private, when everyone predicted he would float it on the stock market, because he believed that shareholders' demands for short-term profits can only undermine long-term strategy in a cyclical business. Smart.

So why did he let in SAS, the first airline to take a stake in BM in 1988 (25% then and a further 15% in 1994)? "They paid the most," says Bishop gnomically. And? Bishop just smiles. He has an unnerving habit of looking straight through you when he thinks he has said enough. Likewise when I ask him if he has ever wanted to get married. "No." Silence. The stare. Best to move on, then.

Most who know him well cannot imagine him handing over control of his airline. It's his life, says one friend; he has no family, plenty of money, he lives for cutting the deals. If he sold or floated, and still hung on at the top, what would he gain? Just someone querying his Savoy expenses.

By the late 90s his own staff were joking that, as BM seems to do something different every decade – 707 charters in the 70s, taking on BA in the 80s, competing with the rest of Europe in the 90s – it might be useful to find out what Bishop plans to do with it after 2000. Will he go head-to-head with the low-cost European operators like Go and EasyJet? No, he says, they don't threaten BM. They will just expand the market as BM itself did in the 80s. Instead his focus has fallen on competing with BA and

Conventio
unconvent

Virgin across the Atlantic. He is rebranding his airline bmi british midland, and preparing to launch a new transatlantic service from Manchester airport. Rivals wonder whether he has left it too late. Bishop's greatest regret, according to one industry source, must be that he didn't take on BA across the Atlantic in the 80s. Look at the size of Virgin Atlantic now.

But direct, head-to-head competition with BA has never been Bishop's style. Even tortoises can get stomped on. Instead he prides himself on building slowly, eschewing ambitious schemes in favour of sensible investment: enhancing revenue growth by putting bigger aircraft on existing routes, that kind of thing. One of the advantages of not being a public company, he says, is that you can ride with low profits for a bit. On the other hand, you could probably raise a lot more money for the investment if you were listed. It's six of one and half a dozen of the other, he concedes.

It would be hard, I guess, to have any kind of row with Bishop. He prides himself on his diplomacy. Apparently, he has an icy temper which he reserves for employees who displease him, but colleagues marvel at his

nal outside
ional inside

ability to keep on good terms with rivals, even those at each other's throats like BA and Virgin. Throughout all the publicity over the "dirty tricks" allegations thrown at BA in the early 90s, for instance, Bishop managed to duck and weave brilliantly to avoid giving offense to either side.

It is this ability to pour oil on troubled waters, and his political instincts, that makes Bishop a popular figure on company boards. As well as being deputy chairman of Airtours he has also been a non-executive director of Williams, the Derby-based multinational that specializes in fire protection and security. Sir Nigel Rudd, Williams' chairman, says Bishop may not be a man who gives much away but he is a very shrewd political operator. "When Michael talks – and remember, he speaks so quietly – everyone leans forward to listen." And he is an intriguing figure, adds Rudd: a private man who is nevertheless a prominent figure in the Midlands, and a wealthy man with a strong streak of sensible parsimony. Not, by any standards, your average, self-made Flash Harry. Nor, on the other hand, the kind of unconventional visionary who sees opportunities where others don't.

Bishop, when asked, sums himself up as "conventional outside, unconventional inside". These contradictions came to the fore when he was asked to chair Channel 4, a job which friends say he was passionate about. He oversaw a sticky patch in the channel's development as it came under fire from the press for the type of programmes it was making, while a Conservative government mulled over the possibility of privatizing it. Blocking that, he says, was his one major contribution to the channel. But hang on, how does he square that with his campaigning for liberalized markets in air travel, and his attacks on the state funding of national carriers?

"Privatization and liberalization have worked very well in the airline and telecoms industries," he says. "They provided consumers with better product at lower cost. Television is different. Channel 4's response to privatization would have been to go down-market which would not have given better product to consumers. You can see the commercial pressures on ITV have been detrimental to the product. My argument was that if they felt a restructuring was needed, they should start with the BBC." And that, apparently, was all he needed to say.

Conventional outside, unconventional inside.

Think about it.

DIVINE ENERGY

Dennis, *like many*
a master of opposites,
the next *bawling*

*entrepreneurs, is
one minute deferential
at a girlfriend*

Felix Dennis hasn't thought about it

"Steadman just done illustration of me, it's absolutely wonderful actually. I
called up Oddbins, found out who his agent was, wrote them. The first sold
seven million, the second one and a half million, they wanted us to do a
third but thought better get out while still had a 1,000 batting average.
Insane price, take them, but only condition that you do picture of me.
Obviously it is in pig mode, unfortunately I sent him photo of me with two
Berkshire pigs, whole theme of this series of drawings is wine-spitting. I
look like a stuck pig spraying blood, don't I? 'Cos he knows my taste in
wine, seen that Granada documentary about me, got Felix Dennis doing
what he does with Chateau Petrus – yeah, I got Petrus – framed it in
wooden binends. Frame done by old friend of mine, been doing my flats
and offices for ever, since Bruce Lee days. Anyway, I've had this place we
are in for about nine years, no reason why I'm here really. Just put pin in

middle of map from Marble Arch, looked for somewhere 100 miles. Went out looking for cottage, found this place. I didn't know I was going to buy it before I walked in the front door. In fact the first time I went past, I needed a pee, there was no-one about, I went into back garden, peed, realized significance of what I had done, marked territory, got back in my Rolls and drove off."

You walk through the door of Felix Dennis's Dorsington Manor and his bristly exuberance just envelopes you. He barely draws breath, he buries you under an avalanche of rant. I can't even remember what we were looking at or what he was talking about – a Steadman illustration? His wine collection? – but he was unstoppable, a burst dam that would flow for hours, a mess of words pouring into my tape recorder.

Which is odd, because his house, a picture-postcard thatched manor south of Stratford, is the opposite of all that. Pin-neat. Hotel-tidy. Full of those fussy flower arrangements and plumped cushions that you get in glossy magazine shoots. Outside, topiaried yew and York stone bake in the summer sun. Inside, oak beams and leaded windows coolly cucoon the antique furniture. Felix Dennis, multimillionaire publisher and ex-hippy, is living an unexpected dream.

But Dennis, like so many entrepreneurs, is a master of polar opposites, one minute deferential and courteous, the next bawling at a girlfriend across the rolling lawn. "BRIN' ME A FUCKING BEER, MARIE-FRANCE!". That summer, when I was sent to meet him, he was not yet 50 but already rich from a business empire that stretched from magazines to computer peripheral sales. Many, though, still remembered him as one of the original three defendants in the Oz trial in 1971, when he, Richard Neville and James Anderson were charged with producing a magazine designed to "corrupt the morals of children". They got sent down, then let off on appeal, spending only a few days in jail but earning lifelong notoriety after the most famous obscenity trial of the 70s.

Back then Dennis, Oz's business manager, told the High Court flatly that money corrupts, man – even though he was already frightening his friends with his aggressive commercial instinct. He also, famously, got a shorter sentence than his co-defendants because the trial judge, Michael Argyle, who was later found to have misdirected the jury, thought he was "less intelligent". Later, when the hundreds of millions of Dennis's business fortune piled up , and the residences in London, Warwickshire, New York, Connecticut and Mustique, and the charitable donations, did he ever offer a rueful smile at Argyle's judgement?

Did he hell. He waited 24 years till Argyle wrote a libellous piece in The Spectator, accusing the Oz team of peddling drugs to schoolchildren, and sued, winning a fulsome apology from the magazine and £10,000 for charity. He didn't pursue Argyle himself as he didn't want to "make him a martyr of the right". But vengeance, at last, was his. Friends said that an important piece of history had been laid to rest, the splinter under the nail of Dennis's achievement removed. He was ready to move on.

And since then his fortune has grown and grown. He has established his group as one of the biggest independent publishers in Britain, and launched his magazine operation into America, where his men's mag *Maxim* has carried all before it. He has confounded those who can't really work out what he does – he never seems to actually run anything, just to have fun – and impressed others with his latest unexpected obsession: to plant tens of thousands of acres he owns in Central England with broadleaved woodland, returning the land to what it was hundreds, maybe thousands of years ago. In other words: reforest Britain. Dennis, if nothing else, is a law unto himself.

The day I walk onto his Dorsington spread it was leaf-burningly hot, up in the 90s, a temperature that seemed to be reducing Dennis to a frazzle. Despite his Panama hat, top-to-toe linen, and wraparound shades, he's sweating profusely. Short, bearded, he harrumphs around his tidy sitting room saying he is going to hit someone because he cannot find the keys to open the windows. He is all fuck-this and fuck-that, cussing and sighing. Rich man blues – you can never find anything if you have too many properties, eh? A fortnight here, a month there...

Next minute he is perking up, talking fast and lewd, like a lubricious satyr, driven along by short bursts of a Gatling gun laugh, and a harder-edged, professorial tone. And all the time he is guzzling: tea, cigarettes, beer, sandwiches, he can't leave his mouth alone. But it's not selfish consolation, he has to share. "Try these, Andrew, try these," he says, again and again. For all his occasionally prickly manner and his awkward egotism – appearing in documentaries about his wealth, pinning copies of his tax cheques to his kitchen wall – Dennis is a quietly generous man, the sort of sentimental millionaire who is touched by the 'and finally' slots on the evening news, and is always sending out money anonymously.

Maybe he feels his wealth is undeserved. Then again, maybe not. When I ask him if he is surprised at how successful he has been, he nearly explodes, thrusting himself forward, trying to intimidate me physically. "And when did you stop beating your wife, eh? Let me ask you the same question? What would you say?

For a moment I think he is going to slug me, completely lose it, then he calms. Just playing. But I had touched a nerve, the twitching point from which the whole performance of exuberance and verve and energy emanates.

Energy: Force or vigour of expression. The exercise of power; active operation, working. Power actively and effectively used. Individual powers in use; activities, exertions. (Latent) ability or capacity to produce an effect. Vigour of action, utterance etc.; a person's capacity for and tendency to strenuous exertion. The ability to do work... (OXFORD ENGLISH DICTIONARY)

Dennis sings the blues, the old manor house, Dorsington, Warwickshire, all his, virtually...

Talk to bosses about their childhoods, their backgrounds, their parents. No-one asks them much about that, you often get it fresh, not reworked by years of recounting as you might with an actor or a politician. That's not to say their answers are totally truthful or even objectively honest, but it is generally honest to how they saw it happen, how they felt it, or at least how they interpret it, now balanced against their current success. How would you answer these kinds of questions? You build up some things, drop others, emphasize maybe what wasn't that important at the time because 30 years on it has a strange resonance. You choose what to tell someone without too much calculation, and if you haven't been asked about it too much before, and experienced how it might be portrayed or misinterpreted in print, you might just tell it how you see it, not how you want it to be seen.

And you listen to a tape of someone like Dennis, or you read the transcript of your notes, and you realize that interpretations of his stories mediate the man too much. You lose the verve. You polish the rawness. You diminish the life. He and his kid brother brought up in post-war London by a single mum tells not the half of it. Because when you talk to him, and he talks to you, it's like winding up wool in a hundred different pieces. You lose the thread, you pick up another, you add yarn over yarn, the ball builds. OK, maybe it's a performance, but it's raw. Just haul it all in.

If you hear me howling

"It's the John Lennon question, isn't it? *How did a git like you get from there to here, right? RIGHT?... RIGHT?...* That's really the question. But yeah, I am surprized and anyone who said they weren't would be a bloody liar.

"And yunno, I had a letter which reminded me of that from a school friend, he had seen the documentary about me, and he wrote and said, you were obsessional when young. I remember my mother made me watch this programme when I was young…"

What programme? His mother or his friend's?

"…and she said, you haven't got any exam results, what are you going to do? Told my mother going to be rich and famous and walked out.

"Was I interested in school work? Nah, I was introduced to what was called race music, which tells you how old I am, by a relative who had travelled abroad to New Orleans. I was 13½, and it was the defining moment of my life. I was doing OK at school, absolutely fine, till then. Now, I always stayed up late. My mother, being an exceptionally wise woman, which she is, not yet a little old lady, she went to bed and I put the singles on the radiogram, and I can tell you what it was, and who it was, and for the next five years of my life, it was who I was.

He breaks into cacophonous shouting-singing.

"IF YOU HEAR ME HOWLING, HOWLING FOR MY DARLING, OOOH-OOH-OOOH-EEEE!"

"I thought, Jesus Christ, the hairs on the back of your neck stand up, and I played it over and over again, and from that moment I was lost. By the time I was 15 I could tell you the difference between southside Chicago and westside, and I could do a passable imitation of half a dozen blues artists. The Stones were just going, but I was an immense snob about them – although any band with Charlie Watts in it can't be all bad. I was obsessed by the blues, I left home, I went to art college.

"I don't want to talk about my family much, my mother has been very hurt by stories about my dad, I'll talk about anything you like but I am not going to injure my mum. The bottom line is that dad left and I was two and a half and that was something in 1950 that was inconceivable. I got into the grammar school and there was one other boy whose parents were divorced. I think my dad's family thought my mum had done him in, but he was in Australia. My mother is beautifully spoken and beautifully dressed and you would never know her background. I think she is foolish for denying it. She married my dad who was upper middle class, a navigator in bombers in the war, he played jazz piano, my mother was incredibly beautiful. He must have woken up with this wife, who had borrowed money to open a tobacconist, and just thought, no. He did write to me and would have explained if I had responded but I didn't. He was an attractive man, and a musician, and what my mother must have thought when she heard me playing IF YOU HEAR ME HOWLING... you can imagine..."

"What did I learn to play?"

He beats out a note-perfect riff on the coffee-table, sweat beading on his brow.

"THAT SPOON THAT SPOON THAT SPOONFUL! Drums and singing. I was a performer. You ever been up on stage? You get up on stage and you got an audience by the bollocks and the band is cooking and you come off that stage and I don't know where the endorphins come from but there is – and I speak from deep experience here – no substitute for that high, no substitute. I wish I could bottle it. I know why Frank Sinatra kept doing it. I was good at it, I did it, and I'm glad I did, but if I had gone on doing it I would be long since dead. And anyway, once I heard myself recorded, it was obvious: I could imitate, but I hadn't got a voice. And there's one rule for a vocalist – you've gotta know it's Rod Stewart, you gotta know it's Ella Fitzgerald. That day I sold the kit and the piano. Which band was I in? I am not going to tell you, loads of bands, but I am not going to bring up any of that shit.

"So I was expelled from school. Why? Absolutely no recollection except I suspect it was for non-attendance and I was a difficult bugger. I have one wonderful recollection from school, a moment which had a profound effect on me. We had a relief teacher with a beard, oh wow man, that was as rare as hens' teeth, a black beard, we called him Abdul. I would dearly like to know where he is now, I heard he went to Scandinavia. He was the English teacher and he continually encouraged me to write more and more stories, and he wrote a comment which I never forgot on something I had written about standing outside a pub not being able to get in. And he wrote; if you keep this up, we will get you in greenback Penguin yet.

"Now, I found writing hard work, immensely hard work, very difficult, and I do rewrite a lot. But I was immensely grateful to him and never forgot it. When I found myself in an environment where writing was important I wasn't... that kind of encouragement meant that, when I knew we had to start a new music section and had to have advertizing, I said I would edit it. And I couldn't have edited a basket of eggs, but I said I could because *he* had said I could.

"University? No, I've honestly never worried about whether everyone else had degrees or not. I am not one of those guys who sits around saying 'I wish I had gone to university'. I tell you what, though, I wish I had gone to university because it's so much fun! Lots of people having leisure, but I didn't, and I probably could have done, so I have no beef about that.

"You'll find when you look at that programme made about me, I've got lots of godchildren and I do give them the library lecture. I take them into the library in whatever home I am in and I say (whisper) 'listen here, you stupid little prick, I have got six other homes like this around the world and all have got libraries bigger than this one, all full of books, and I still haven't caught up yet, so you can either do it the easy way or you can do it my way...' Hahahaha! Yeah, the easy way is to go to university, and the purpose of the exercise is to persuade them to stay in school and go to college. Even though life sometimes proves the opposite.

"You think I'm too blunt? Well, that's why they love your's truly, because I talk to them as adults, and I laugh at my own advice and they see me laughing, and I add, don't take any notice of people telling you things, but it is easier if you've been to college, it gives you confidence, doesn't it? Cor, try these sandwiches.

"Do a lot of people stay here? As with most of my residences, people come and stay and go, and sometimes I don't even know they have been here. Do I feed them? Yeah. Expect them to bring a present? No, but I collect wine, thanks. Wife, girlfriend? I am not married and not going to get married, I'm not jealous or territorial. You know, my first reaction on seeing a really great new rival magazine is not, oh shit, but good on you son, this is fucking great!

"Tempted to have children? No – do you know how many hairless monkeys there are? I am gutless, I haven't got the courage. How these people can just casually have children, which if they are any kind of responsible human being, will utterly transform their life for ever is totally beyond me. I just connect, because I know it would take over my life.

"And yeah, I have felt my own mortality. You're looking at the only survivor of Legionnaire's Disease you will ever see. Got it in the USA in '88 or '89. I thought I had the world's worst flu... doctor kept shaking me and saying, it's really simple, you've over 40 years old, you obviously smoke, you drink like a fish and probably take illegal drugs, you have contracted legionella and if you go to sleep you are probably going to die.

"Did I change? No, but it's all a bonus now. I don't work so what do I do? My mum keeps asking me when I am going to get a proper job, but I am just doing what you will be doing in 30 years' time. I just do one thing at a time. My guiding business principle is that I know a man who can and I let them get on with it. Occasionally I think they are going off the rails, there's always something in my universe that urgently needs my attention. Now,

I'll tell you about a new product and you tell me whether you think it's a good idea, but promise you won't write about it... Wait till you see this, it will knock your fucking socks off..."

Michael Grade was in therapy

Men and parents, part 365. Talking to Michael Grade, chairman of Pinewood Studios, former boss of Channel 4: he is exuberant, charming, driven, a connector and communicator, one of the best people managers in media. He hasn't spoken to his mother since she left his father when Michael was two; he cut off his sister after a bust-up as teenagers. He has a string of failed personal relationships behind him. He acknowledges in his autobiography that he spent six years in therapy while running Channel 4 trying to sort himself out. Sitting in his first-floor office at Pinewood, we had the following conversation:

Does he think the six years in therapy have made him less ambitious?

He frowns. No, he says. "It changed me in my private life. It didn't change me as a manager."

How can you separate the two?

"Because intimate relationships require different levels of maturity. I have always been very good at understanding the dynamic in relationships at work, but hopeless at home."

Is that because he is better at dealing with men?

"No."

Did therapy encourage him to rebuild the breaches with his mother and sister?

"No," he says.

Is his mother still alive?

He stifles a yawn. "I believe so."

Don't friends think it is odd that he can cut others out of his life like that?

He is so gregarious and eager-to-please, it seems almost jarringly out of character. It is also something that his critics (including the *Daily Mail*, who ruthlessly tracked down his mother nine years ago and asked her, 'how do you feel?') frequently use against him. Wouldn't it be easier to resolve it?

"There's nothing to resolve. People are always curious but they can only apply their experience to mine, and it is not relevant to mine. It is not a matter of judgement, it's just the way the cards are dealt, that's all. I don't feel a void in my life."

You don't care about the money?

Dennis is still talking, rapping away like he's being paid millions per word per minute.

"Am I good with figures? Ha! No I'm terrible, I can't understand a balance sheet and I am not joking, but I can spot anomalies and that's important. Why do I want to set up in America? Because that's where the big boys play, that's the belly of the beast. I went there early with the one-shots, we're the only major publishing company that has got a one-shot division. I don't care about the money, I never did, that gives me a tremendous advantage. I don't know how much I am worth nor does anyone else. Share prices might have something to do with it, but I've got an awful lot of real estate and an awful lot of art."

"D'ya know, I was given the opportunity of becoming American? I was interviewed by a very enterprising gentleman from the IRS there, I thought I had done something wrong. He said I didn't need a lawyer, I said, right, here's my lawyer, and then I said, I don't understand what I have done wrong, I pay my taxes under the double taxation treaty. And he said, no, no, why do you like paying tax? I said, I don't like paying tax. He said, so why don't you become an American citizen and pay a lot less?

He stuffs his mouth full of sandwich.

"I thought, bloody hell, he's bloody touting for business! This is the difference between Britain and America, man.

"I said, that means I have to become an American citizen. He says, exactly. I said, but I'm English, man. He said, we appreciate that, why don't you just take an American passport and be English in your heart?

"Hahaha! Son of a bitch! I thought that was great. I keep copies of all my tax cheques on the wall, I'll show you if you want, come on..."

We march to the kitchen where he points out framed cheques for varying sums: £900,000, £2m.

"Am I happy? Oh, God, what a question! Come on! People want me to say I'm miserable. I AM NOT MISERABLE, MAN! You know, I have lived and continue to live the life of Reilly. I have all my life, I have never clocked in, I have never said yes, sir, in my life. I don't wake up feeling miserable. I do whatever I fucking want every day of my life and it isn't the money. I did the same without the money.

"But do I need others to clock in to maintain my empire? AMEN TO THAT! HAHAHA!"

He laughs, spraying crumbs, wildly, maniacally.

"Yeah, but in my defence I will say I do go round..."

He pauses, clearly trying to think what his defence is.

"Yunno, the older I get, the more I love talent, I fucking love talent, and I wish it well. People who want to start on their own, I give them money to start on their own. Good luck to them."

And it's true. He does.

Two lines by Alexander Pope (on Dryden)

The varying verse, the full resounding line,
The long majestic march, and energy divine.

Riding in a yellow Bentley

A few years later I am driven across Knightsbridge in a bright yellow
Bentley by a large, 24-year-old Sikh who was once listed as Britain's
youngest self-made millionaire. While he drives, he is enthusing: about his
new businesses, about his car, about life in general. The traffic parts almost
in deference to his pent-up energy. It is a Felix Dennis moment.

Tony Blair's favourite young entrepreneur

It's arranged: Reuben Singh will meet me at London's Hilton hotel, Park
Lane. You can't miss him, says his office, he'll be in his yellow Bentley,
personalized number plate, and sure enough, there he is, standing outside
the hotel in the spring sunshine beside the brightest car this side of a lemon
on wheels.

"Do you like it?" asks Singh, instantly chummy. "I got it last week. It's the
only one of its type in the world!"

And you can believe it. It's gleamy new, £270,000-worth of eyepopping
status symbol with walnut dashboard, black leather seats edged in yellow
piping and a Sikh Khanda symbol dangling from the mirror. Singh himself
is in designer Sikh mode: black trousers, black boots, black rollneck, black
turban and bushy black beard tucked into his sweater. It's all rather surreal.

Anyway, he says, he can't park the Bentley here, it won't fit in the NCP
downstairs (!), let's go to the Sheraton Tower, he'll leave it there. He gives

Singh made his firs
doing his

the impression that he doesn't really want to let it out of his sight, and at that price, who can blame him?

So off we go, tooling through the Knightsbridge traffic, Singh clearly rather enjoying his new toy, rabbiting away, me sitting up front wishing I was in the back giving a regal wave.

"Oh hi, yellow," says the doorman at the Sheraton when Singh throws him the keys. You don't forget a car like that, I guess. We settle in the hotel bar, the car still winking at us in the sunlight through the plate-glass front of the building. Singh doesn't want to use his apartment round the corner for the interview, or any of his offices. Actually, I can't really make out if Singh, who's based in Manchester, has an office in London, or indeed an apartment, as he tends to talk in a vague way, and getting concrete answers out of him is sometimes a bit difficult. There may be good reason for this, as I found out later, but for now, let's just say I enjoyed his warm garrulousness without quibble.

fortune while still
A *levels*

What's indisputable, though, is that Singh, one-time retailer, now currency trader and dotcom owner, is the highest-profile young entrepreneur in town these days. And by young, I mean young. Still not 25, Singh made his first fortune out of a chain of over 100 jewellery and accessories shops called Miss Attitude which he set up while still doing his A levels. Yes, it helped that his parents run a large Manchester-based wholesaler, Sabco, which supplies a string of major retail outlets, but it was still an astonishing feat.

He sold his shops in 1999 and moved onto other things, since when estimates of his wealth, and indeed his success, have varied. His profile, however, has remained on a high and seems to have convinced the government, always on the lookout for an amenable entrepreneur, that he is a horse worth backing. And with his pedigree – young, smart and Asian – it's not hard to see why. After meeting Tony Blair in 1999, Singh was invited onto both the DTI's competitiveness council and its small business council, and was appointed one of the country's five ambassadors for entrepreneurship (along with the likes of Sir Alan Sugar and Sir Richard Branson). He was also chosen to serve on the 'peer reviews' that report on government departments.

That's quite some approval rating and may also, perhaps, have something to do with the fact that Singh's family is close to Lord Paul, the Labour multimillionaire steel boss. And when not sitting on government committees and, presumably, running his new ventures, Singh has worked hard to keep up that profile: he is a frequent speaker at conferences, on panels, to venture capital gatherings and the like. Everybody, it seems, wants a slice of him – after all, young entrepreneurs are so *hot* – and, as a proficient performer, he clearly loves it.

And he *is* very convincing. Meet Singh and you can see why the politicians have such confidence in him: pearly smile, loquacious tongue, turban and beard giving him a gravitas that belies his youth. He also combines warmth and wit with a winning detachment from his own, rather flash exterior. In fact, he makes it all sound totally logical – you make a lot of money, hence you get a yellow Bentley. Why not? It's fun.

So there we are, sitting in an empty bar in the early afternoon, Singh drinking mineral water – he's teetotal – talking nineteen to the dozen, as is his wont. He tells me about his latest venture, an e-business called alldayPA.com, an internet-based, virtual office service that offers data storage, webspace, secretarial services, online personal organizers and more to the harassed owners of today's small businesses. Basically, he says, it provides all the back-up that he lacked when he was first starting up.

"It stems from the problems I had starting my first business at 17. I had no back-office, no infrastructure. I kept quiet about it because it was embarrassing but when I got involved with the DTI, I saw it was not just my problem but every small business has these problems. I knew I had to create something that could give small business the weapon or the tools to compete against big business."

If that sounds almost philanthropic, it isn't. It is designed to make a profit. Singh was looking particularly pleased with himself when we met as he had just sold 10% of the business to an Arizona-based technology fund for £10.5m. That values his stake at over £80m – he reckons to have spent only £3m setting it up over the past two years, so hence, perhaps, the reward of the bright yellow Bentley. The launch of the business also means he gets to spend more time in the US, which he clearly loves. He intimates that eventually he may even move there.

That would mean leaving Manchester, of course, but my guess is he could handle that. The city was the base chosen by his parents when they emigrated here from India in the early 70s. Why Manchester? Because that is where his father had come in the 60s to get his MBA. Both his mother and father were graduates from business families in Delhi who, according to Singh, married for love, rather than follow the tradition of an arranged marriage, and were determined to seek a new life elsewhere. They knew no-one in Manchester, no family, no links, and put everything into making a success of themselves there, first by setting up a manufacturing business, then a jewellery import operation.

How Reuben Singh was formed

As you would expect, Singh cites his parents as the key influences in his business life. What are they like? His father, says Singh, is "the thinker", his mother "the driving force". She handles sales in their firms, deals with the large UK clients, has the good communication skills. "I am much more like her," says Singh. "We are very close."

Everything in his parents' lives revolves around business. Their choice of prep school for their two sons was determined by the fact that it operated

Reuben Singh

7am–6pm, leaving more time clear for work. Outside of school, however, they would take their children with them everywhere, out to dinner, away to friends; they wouldn't accept invitations unless the children could come too. This was partly because they had no extended family to support them, but it also meant the boys grew up faster, their lives dominated by the same obsessions as their parents.

So the things Singh remembers most about growing up is listening to his parents talk about prospects over the dinner table, or doing his homework in the room set aside for the boys at the office, or playing football in the loading bays of the warehouse. When he was older, Singh would accompany his mother on her sales trips to the Far East, studying how business was done. "Reuben has the same drive as his parents," says Anisha Sawhney, a family friend. "They treated him on the same level as themselves, they trusted him from an early age, and that makes you grow up earlier." Hence his extraordinary maturity.

But it was Singh's local shopping trips, every Saturday in Manchester with his mother, that gave him the kernel for his first business idea. "You know what it's like going shopping with a woman," says Singh, eyes flashing. "You go from shop to shop, guys can get everything from one shop, why do women have to go to so many? And Asian women are really into jewellery, so we would be going to one shop for jewellery, one shop for make-up, one for accessories – handbags, watches, purses. I said to mum 'why can't you get it all from one store?' and she said, 'because none exists that sells them all'."

Which led Singh to thinking 'why not?'. So, as he tells it, he canvassed his friends at grammar school, thought the idea of a shop that sold it all was pretty neat, sorted out some suppliers, tried to get a site in Manchester's Arndale Centre and was told by the manager to stop wasting his time. This made him twice as determined. He went to the public library, read the retail trade magazines, worked out that you could go through property agents, convinced one he was serious and got him to secure the first site (in the Arndale Centre – ya boo sucks to the manager). Then Singh fitted it, filled it, named it, opened it and did so well that within a month he had opened another Miss Attitude. And another, and another. And this was before he had even taken his A levels.

"I was forced by my dad to stop after three shops because of my exams, but I was already employing 30 people! The market was crying out for more and I was forced to stop!" he laughs.

Why did it take off? Because, he says, being a kid, he was able to create a place where young kids wanted to go. "We'd break all the rules about music on full-blast, turn it into a disco, we were dragging so many people through the doors – 3,000 people on a Saturday – that the shopping centres loved us." And being a premature adult, he was able to run it efficiently, source good stock, negotiate more property deals and roll out his chain to a template.

Eventually, exams under his belt, he could concentrate on that roll-out, while simultaneously reading business studies at Manchester Metropolitan University. By the time he came to selling up, he had over 100 shops, plus spin-off companies handling shopfitting, manufacturing and currency trading. Why currency trading? Because Singh got annoyed at not getting the best rates when he was buying overseas. Likewise shopfitting and manufacturing. If you can't get a good price, do it yourself.

It's a pretty extraordinary story for someone not yet 20. How deeply were his parents involved? Not at all, he says, his father was against the plan from the start and wouldn't even act as guarantor with the suppliers, though clearly his trade connections helped. Others back that up. "They were supportive," says Sanjay Dhir, the Leeds-based entrepreneur whose Time Design company supplied watches to Miss Attitude. "But what Reuben is doing is different. They weren't in retail, and they are certainly not in IT."

In fact, Singh describes Miss Attitude almost as an act of rebellion: his father had wanted him to stick to the family business, and had eased him in, letting him handle sales while still at school. He had also given him the kind of perks that would wed him to the job, including a £40,000 BMW for his 17th birthday (this from a father who Singh describes as "very conservative" – though clearly he has a romantic streak too: he wanted to call his eldest son Ruby until his Jewish neighbours suggested Reuben might be a kinder choice).

Singh, however, found that the perks just made his own friends resentful. That was what made him so determined to set up on his own: to prove he could do it himself. He even gave the car back. "Dad thought I had gone berserk," he laughs, "but I wanted to do things my own way so people would see it was my success, not my father's."

So he built up Miss Attitude. By 1999 he had 1,000 employees and was talking openly about his aims for 500 stores. There was also talk of flotation and diversification – in fact, talk about everything, which, I have discovered since, is what some feel Singh's real strength is.

The art of profile part two

Conference speaker, youngest self-made millionaire in the Guinness Book of Records, portrait in the National Portrait Gallery, all those government advisory roles – sometimes you get the feeling that Reuben Singh's PR is almost bigger than the achievements that warranted them in the first place.

Which is the way it is, of course, with young entrepreneurs in the post-Branson age: Singh sells himself hard, a trait that doesn't surprise his business contemporaries. "With all entrepreneurs," shrugs Dhir, "30% is achievement, and 70% is personal marketing."

70%?

With all entrepreneurs,

and **70%** *is*

No wonder a few who've dealt with Singh are rather sceptical about his claims.

There are, for instance, certain blank spots that you can't get information on. "I would be very surprised if you can find anything on paper about his companies or how much money he has," says one who has researched Singh. Even when Singh sold the Miss Attitude chain to Klesch Capital in early 1999, it was very unclear how much money he made from the transaction. Was it £50m or was it £22m? Or did he, as one newspaper surmised, only walk away with £500,000?

Ask him and Singh becomes uncharacteristically tight-lipped. "We sold the company on a non-disclosure agreement for between £500,000 and £50m. The non-disclosure agreement lasts for four years. Only thing I will say is that within a month, I'd incorporated two companies with £7m in them."

30% is achievement, personal marketing.

Yet the last records filed in Companies House for Miss Attitude show a firm making a profit of only around £300,000 on a £4m turnover, and carrying debt. Maybe it wasn't as successful as everyone thought? Gary Klesch, founder of Klesch Capital, doesn't want to talk about it either. Why not? Won't say.

All very mysterious and it begs the question: have we got to the stage where entrepreneurs exaggerate everything to create their own mythology?

Yes.

So why did Singh sell? The chain had simply ceased to be the main focus of his interest, he says, and he wanted to move onto other projects. Would he ever go back? "I have done retail now, no challenge in it," he says.

Actually, his first thought after selling was of retiring – at 22! – and living off the interest of his capital. He planned a five-month holiday in America, but it lasted little more than a week because he got so bored. Instead, he went to Palo Alto in Silicon Valley and started looking for new opportunities, just as the e-business bubble was pumping up. He could feel the excitement. Hence, in the spring of 2001, the launch of alldayPA.com. Wrong time to launch a dotcom, after the bubble has burst? No, he says, he loves going against trends.

What motivates him, then? Profile? Cash? Cars?

Not really, he says, just "keeping busy". So he runs his various projects (38 companies set up), juggling ideas, looking for options, "It's in his blood," says one friend. "He's a player like everyone else and he wants to win. And the more he wins, the more he wants to play."

In that he is no different to his parents, and his younger brother Bobby, who ran Singh's shopfitting business before branching out on his own. It's a whole dynasty of entrepreneurs. And they all still live together in the family home in Manchester, well, nominally at least, as Singh has promised his parents he will keep a base there but is often travelling somewhere else. Yes, he says, he does want to move to America (has he told Tony Blair?), but only if he can persuade his parents to come too, and they are keen, apparently.

Is that because America is a better place for entrepreneurs? No, he says, stroking the top of his beard, I don't think I could have succeeded anywhere else but Britain.

That's not answering the question.

OK, he says, if they move, it will be because of three reasons: weather, women and... "Help me, I'm looking for another W". Finally, he gets one. "Wealth, they are not so jealous of wealth in America." A big chuckle emerges from the beard. "See how great I am, I thought of three!"

Women? I thought he had said he wanted to marry a Sikh? There has been much speculation in the past about his love life, about how he had sacrificed girlfriends for business success, with the hint that he was probably a bit of a mummy's boy – he says so himself. Why does he need to go to America to find love?

"You find me an Asian girl in this country. I've looked."

Does she have to be Asian?

"Culturally," he says, "I think it is important."

He has, he continues, become more religious since he has been successful. He recently got baptized near the Golden Temple in Amritsar, India, spiritual home of the Sikh religion. He doesn't drink, doesn't smoke, doesn't eat meat and is now a stricter observer of Sikh religious practices than his parents. He has stopped cutting his beard as well as his hair. So, a Sikh wife is best.

How long is his hair?

Actually, he laughs, most of it is dropping out, he's probably going bald like his father. Ha! His dark eyes twinkle. And later, when we have moved outside for the photoshoot, Singh is still geniality itself. He poses against a wall, squats down by his beloved car. He looks every inch the star, passers-by admire the Bentley, even ask for his autograph. Just before he leaves, he asks if we could blur the car's number plate in the pictures. Sorry? Oh, he's had a couple of threats in the past – like any high-profile businessman, he is vulnerable to cranks, doesn't want to be too visible.

When he leaves, Harry and I turn to each other and ask, so why buy a bright yellow Bentley with a personalized plate?

What we mean, of course, is why is he trying so hard? It doesn't have to be like that. There is such a thing as laid-back energy too…

his mischievous, grey wandering *body that enters*

To make you envious

April 2000: I am sitting on a beach in Turks and Caicos with Butch Stewart, founder of the Sandals resort chain and one of the travel trade's best-known entrepreneurs. Stewart, nearly 60, white Jamaican with British roots, is the hardest-working man in the West Indies. Air Jamaica? He owns it, he sorted it out. Tourists? Up to half a million a year go through his resorts. Money? He's supposed to bring more currency into Jamaica than any other operator.

Pinning him down to an interview had been murder. Just turn up, his people say, he'll see you. But where? Jamaica? Maybe, they say, if he's not somewhere else. Antigua, St Lucia, the Bahamas, Miami, or even Milwaukee. Stewart is always on the move, forever checking business or pressing flesh. No-one has more energy, no-one puts himself about more. Eventually it's decided: it has to be Turks and Caicos – a string of islands

eyes *keep to the next* **bikinied** *his sightline*

north of Cuba – because he has invited all the tour operators there for a party to launch a new resort. Hell, in my line of work you have to make sacrifices. Turks it is then.

But keeping Stewart's attention is hard. He's a big teddy-bear of a man, paunchy, engaging, with all parts working. We're sipping Diet Cokes on the veranda of his surfside fish restaurant and his mischievous, grey eyes keep wandering to the next bikinied body that enters his sightline.

"Aah," he sighs as two women, leggy French travel agents, sashay beneath us. "Those legs man… HELLO LADIES, HOW'S PARIS?" he shouts. They smile politely. Stewart, I should point out here, has been married and divorced twice and opts for a typically Caribbean frankness when it comes to the opposite sex.

He speaks in a Jamaican patois which his staff says gets thicker the closer he is to his home island. The son of a Jamaican radio engineer with ties to

Britain – his grandfather fought in the Royal Flying Corps in the First World War – he got his nickname (he was christened Gordon) from an American sailor when he was small. The name stuck. Now he runs one of the biggest business empires in the Caribbean, having built up a near-billion dollar holiday group on the back of his resort and airline operation. That includes brand names like Sandals (ten resorts and counting) and Beaches (aimed at families) – both run as "all-inclusives" where everything is paid for up-front – and Air Jamaica, as well as stakes in a newspaper, media outfits and a host of other ventures.

In cash-strapped Jamaica, currently wrestling with the IMF after decades of financial mismanagement by successive governments, Stewart's resort operation alone makes him a very powerful economic and political force. But for you and me he is just Mr Sandals, the man behind those rather kitschy ads, all bosomy blondes and happy hunks, that seem to run on every dismal London Underground train.

Why couples?

"It was a no-brainer," says Stewart, chinking the ice in his glass. "Just look around the back of any aeroplane, who do you see travelling? Couples. It was obvious." He started with one hotel in Montego Bay, tried a few ideas till he got it right, then just rolled it out from there. And the name? Nothing to do with sandals coming in pairs and all the other myths, it was a beach thing, he says, suggested by a friend of his. He had hated it at first but it grew on him…

Why has he been so successful?

Simply, say others, because of his energy and his organizational skills, and because he is very good at the resort business. Ironic, really, when you think that he only went into it to raise foreign currency so he could import materials for his appliance and air conditioner firms – "Jamaican dollars were no use then," he shrugs. But he swiftly discovered he had a gift for hotels. Now everyone in the travel trade knows Butch, probably because he has given out more freebies to tour operators and journalists than just about any resort boss going. He realized early on, he says, that profile is everything and if people hadn't actually been to his resorts, they would be filled with misconceptions.

And he's got that aggressive will-to-win common to all great entrepreneurs. He goes on about how he flunked off school, messing around on the beach when he was a kid, and how he's really a square – "I've never tried drugs, I learnt all that from my mum, she frowns on those kinds of things in a big way" – but you know that under the laid-back charm there's a killer edge.

Educated in Jamaica, with two years at a crammer in swinging London thrown on top, Stewart uses his island nonchalance to mask a real need to prove himself. His parents never had a lot of money, but they knew how to entertain people, especially his father, Daddy Stew, who still turns up in Butch's office at the age of 83. "He's a joker, an entertainer," smiles Stewart. Some of that rubbed off. Despite the money made from the appliance businesses, it's in the travel trade that Stewart has really excelled because, say those who work with him, he understands how to keep people happy.

For instance, he is credited with transforming Air Jamaica since a desperate government begged him to take it off them, simply by banging heads together, getting experienced executives in, providing proper funding and giving customers what they wanted: a reliable service in aeroplanes that didn't look like they went out of commission with the ark, and fun – which Butch is something of a master at orchestrating.

So Air Jamaica has fashion shows, in-seat aerobics, free champagne but most importantly... "on time, no lines," says Stewart, grinning that grin. Plus, of course, it suited him to get control of the means of shipping his

banks were
at him to fund

customers in, so he's a happy man too. Locals compare his style to Richard Branson's: ruthlessly entrepreneurial but with an eye to PR which generates a strangely awe-struck reverence. Like Branson, Butch never gives up when he meets an obstacle, one Bahamian told me, shaking his head. He just finds another way of achieving his end.

Added to which, Stewart is a great organizer. His empire is a supreme exercise in logistics. With ten Sandals, four Beaches and a clutch of cheaper Sandals Inns, he has thousands of tourists moving through his resorts every week. The key to the resorts' popularity is the quality. "In the mid-80s people thought we were some kind of holiday camp, man, with long lines for buffet food, but we changed all that." Good restaurants, huge pools, giant Jacuzzis, ritzy spas, lots of waterskiing, free scuba, endless events organized (the volleyball, the discos, the ping-pong competitions, the weddings).

thrusting cash

the expansion

Stewart says he based it on Club Med, but with a twist. None of that Gallic froideur, lots of Jamaican sass and rather more home comforts than you might expect. They are not cheap (expect to pay £1200 plus for a week including flights), but he's got the good beaches – Negril, the north coast of Providenciales in Turks, Dickenson Bay in Antigua – and an organizational set-up that works.

That includes, at his massive new Beaches resort in Turks (capacity: around 1,000 guests), shipping in container-loads of soil to plant the bougainvillea and cypresses in, chefs and service staff to run nine quality restaurants, diving experts to train great gangs of tourists to scuba in a morning. It goes on and on. Now Stewart has a template, he can set up anywhere, and, when we met, banks were thrusting cash at him to fund the expansion. Because while America, his main market, and the UK were in boom time, the business just rolled in. Sure, he's worked hard at it, shaking just about every tour operator's hand from Miami to Montreal. But it's paid off. They love him.

"The thing about Butch," one American travel writer explained to me, while the Stewart launch party in Turks was in full swing and we were all knee-deep in his legendary hospitality, "is that in a part of the world where everything seems disorganized, he can organize anything."

Butch Stewart's no-problem attitude

So where's he get the energy? Stewart says he doesn't know. His father was a radio engineer, his mother ran a small appliance business. Maybe he got his charm from the former, his drive from the latter. "School was bumpy, I was not good academically. I was at boarding school from young, not heavily supervised so spent a lot of time on the reef. I have a lot of friends who have the same problem in Jamaica. There is so much of this kind of life." He gestures along the beach. "It's a big distraction, it's so easy not to work."

Then he smiles.

"But I honestly don't think I've worked a day in my life. To get paid to do all the things you like so much... There's no question about it: if you like what you are doing, then you have a focus about something and, yunno, you have a feel for it."

He talks me through setting up his first hotel resort, in Montego Bay, the mistakes he made, how he learnt on site, how he built what he learnt into programmes to train and motivate his staff, to make sure all his operatives have the same 'no-problem' attitude to customer demands. And how he learnt that nothing is better than just being there, whether it is touring his resorts or seeing the travel agents across Europe and America.

"You have to know how to make the product work and you have to know how to sell it. If you don't know where to sell it, then you are not going to sell anything. That takes practice and experience, and walking the streets of New York and Milwaukee and Timbuctoo and talking to people and showing them what you have. I have travelled all over Europe doing that. Some of the people listen to you. Some don't."

And the other important thing is to know your limits. There'd been speculation that he might push his resort concept outside the Caribbean but he denies it. To do that, he says, he would have to franchise it out, and he doesn't want to do that. "If you start over-reaching you lose your service and then you lose your standards and that's what it's all about. If we became global, we'd have to lower our aim."

No, he continues, he may do cruise ships, and he's got some land in the Dominican Republic, he'll build there, "Mexico is probably attractive to us too," he says, turning to ogle another woman walking by, pursing his lips. I am beginning to think maybe I should hose him down, then I remember one of his PRs saying that the longest interview Butch ever gave was to a blonde female reporter so, failing a sex change and a bottle of bleach, at least I've got him in a good spot with plenty of visuals.

He giggles when I ask him if he has a girlfriend right now. "I am officially single," he grins, "but I'm best friends with me ex-wives." Of his four kids, one already works for the company and the others "can't wait". A fifth, his eldest son, died in a car crash ten years ago.

So would he say he's had women problems? "Oh I don't know why the marriages went wrong, just one of those things." He says it's easier running his business as a single guy. "Yunno, I have to travel all round the Caribbean, I like the freedom, I don't have to get up and explain why I'm going or ask if they want to come too. I do enjoy it. Every so often you feel you're in a cage and can't get out, yunno?"

And he has a great life. A house in Kingston, another in Montego Bay, another in Miami, a London bolthole in Chelsea. Then there are the Jaguars and Mercedes he drives and the big boats. This May, he says, he is going to take the whole month off and go fishing in the Bahamas, live on his boat, try and get some of that fat off his stomach. "Too many aeroplane rides, too much moving around," he says, slapping his stomach. "I tell you, spend six weeks on the boat, cook fish every morning, the weight drops right off..."

Then he's going to London to watch some cricket. Butch will have a box, everyone's invited, it will be one hell of a party. And you don't doubt that it will, because a lot of Stewart's life is about organizing permanent party-time. He's so good at it. The other part, of course, like the duck of legend, is about keeping those little legs going furiously beneath the water-line, managing the expansion, flesh-pressing the travel agents, monitoring the staff, walking the beaches, planning the future, having the discipline to keep pushing on, never easing up.

Retirement? Nah, he says, eyes flitting, just checking who's coming past, "I'm having so much fun..."

DRIVEN DISCIPLINE

Did I mention discipline?

Discipline is the trait that people forget, that everyone under-rates. Ask Sir Alan Sugar, founder of Amstrad. Observers remark on his drive, his aggression, his uncouth lack of charm. But ask him why he has been successful and he will say…

"Discipline, a lot of that, you have to discipline yourself when you are working for yourself. There's no-one else to report to on a Monday morning."

Discipline yourself to put in the hours, to make the deals, to push through the programmes, to keep wages down, to keep energy high, not to bunk off, not to give up, not to pay yourself so much that you stop trying at the first sign of success.

Every week, says Sugar, when he started, he learnt to discipline himself to work hard so that by Wednesday, he'd earned the salary he needed. After that, it was pure profit.

And then later, discipline yourself to keep pushing on, to remain competitive, to stay committed, not to lose sight of the goals.

But what about luck?

Sugar leans forward, his face squished up like a wrinkled pickled onion. "There is no luck involved in my business success, I have got to tell you that."

> *Discipline: controlled and orderly behaviour resulting from training. The system of order and strict obedience to rules enforced among pupils, soldiers or others under authority.* (OXFORD ENGLISH DICTIONARY)

One afternoon in the West End with Sir Alan Sugar

I am waiting for Sugar when he walks into his Mayfair apartment block. He is shorter than I expect, neater – spotless blue suit, precision-trimmed beard and hair – and shyer. We are introduced, he shakes hands sparingly, never makes eye contact, barely looks up. The lift takes us to the sixth floor, a vast penthouse duplex overlooking Green Park, and he mumbles, see you later, I'll be upstairs, you can wait.

Right. If I didn't know his middle name was Michael, as in Alan Michael Sugar Trading (Amstrad), I'd know for certain it was Gruff.

That's the man's image, and he likes to live up to it. Spend around 15 minutes in his presence, and you are quickly reduced to the role of timid flunky, hoping to catch his eye (unlikely), worrying that you may be displeasing him, trying to avoid the verbal bollocking that, when we finally got round to talking, he started giving his Amstrad e-mailer.

He called the 2000

years

"SHIT!" he shouts. "The fucking phone's gone blue-screen again! Are you serious? It's unbelievable! Unbelievable!"

When he is not expressing exasperation, he gives off the kind of silent, simmering discontent that can easily be misread as contempt. In the two hours I was around him I didn't see him smile once. Not once. No wonder he has a reputation as a tough man to work for. Rarely have I met a boss who is *so* ungiving.

Which is a shame because he's no fool. At 54, he has already built a £500m-plus personal fortune out of his ability to buy and sell brilliantly: radios, hi-fis, computers, anything. He has a genius for spotting what consumers want and knows how to get it to them at a price. And when he allows himself to be, he is a funny, perspicacious commentator on the British business scene. He's famously coruscating about both the duplicity of City advisers and the venality of ad agencies, to name just two targets.

But most of all, he's good at making money. He called the 2000 tech stock crash years before it happened, he was quietly piling into property before

tech stock crash
before it happened

Alan Sugar

people recognised it was an adroit switch – the Mayfair duplex we are in, for example, is not his home (he would never, say his friends, live in somewhere as flash as that), just a block he is doing up and selling. The enormous penthouse, in which we sit, is on the market for £8.5m, bit beyond my budget. It's also more than Sugar paid for the whole building.

He was even set to get out of Tottenham Hotspur, the football club with which he has been entwined for nearly a decade, with more money than he started. That would be a first for many football club chairmen. Of course, he cannot crow about it. "It will alienate people," he says gravely, as if he cares. But the facts are there: paid £8m for his stake, sold two-thirds of it to Tottenham's new owner ENIC for £22m, still holds 13%. We met on the day before ENIC disposed of George Graham, Sugar's controversial pick as Spurs manager, so who knows what he thought of that? Only later was it revealed that Sugar was just as exasperated with the underachieving Graham as he was with the rest of the soccer world he was always ranting about: overpaid players, grasping agents, lying press, moaning fans.

Imagine my surprise at the time, then, when Sugar tells me he has mellowed.

"Yeah, I've mellowed," he says, "definitely, no question of it." Hence the efforts "to put something back" in recent years. He's been lecturing to students about entrepreneurialism, at the government's request – picture that ten years ago – and handing out money to good causes: £1.3m to the Hackney Empire theatre only two months before. This from a man not noted for his interest in Britain's cultural scene. It was roots, he says. He's Hackney born and bred, he used to buy fish and chips next door to the Empire.

He speaks quickly, economically, his growling East End rasp now softened with age. Or perhaps it's all that putting-about he's doing. Knighthood, Buckingham Palace, Downing Street functions, those lecture tours. If I was a little cynical I would think there is a bit of remodelling going on here, not entirely unconnected with the fact that Sugar's biggest company Learning Technology, part of Viglen plc, is now the largest supplier of computer equipment to schools…

It's the sort of hint that could get you a swipe from some interviewees but Sugar likes to get as good as he gives. "Ha!" he shouts. "If only it were that simple!" No, he's not cosying up to government, he just wants to encourage entrepreneurialism, he thinks we are good at it and he knows it provides people with a way out.

Really? He says he's always surprised by what people read into his actions. Trying to take Amstrad private in 1992 was seen by shareholders as getting control on the cheap (they rejected his plan, he later broke the company up, then renamed another firm Amstrad). Likewise buying into Tottenham in 1991 was interpreted as a smart step to get inside a business which Sugar, the satellite dish manufacturer, knew was going to boom. Or was he sent in by Rupert Murdoch to mole the negotiations for television rights?

"Nah, absolute rubbish," he says. "From an ego point of view I would love to say how clever I am, but it's got nothing to do with that." Buying into Tottenham was about saving the club his dad loved. "And a lot of the community stuff I do, I don't make a fuss about. I have built schools and old age homes and supported Great Ormond Street." (In all, he's donated over £4.5m since 1986).

The truth is, he is so good at making money that people don't believe he could give it away without getting some edge or personal benefit.

He's not sure where he got that money-making nous from – not his dad, who was a factory tailor, nor his mum, who stayed at home looking after the family. But he thinks that much of his character and motivations were formed by his circumstances. So we start with that.

Lawyers allowing...

Sir Alan Sugar sits at a small round table in a long, wood-panelled study. The room is spotless, characterless, part of the cavernous, beige, penthouse suite that is up for sale. He scowls slightly, grumpily, avoiding eye contact, making clear any conversation is going to be like a long hike up an icy slope.

Tell me about your upbringing.

"My parents were very much working class people, my father was a tailor in the east end of London, brought up in the mould of go to work in a factory and that's how the whole family was brought up. We were English back three generations, before that Russian or Polish, but I don't feel an iota of that now. Basically we lived in a council flat in Clapton in Hackney, the whole family was factory oriented, we worked in the garment industry in the days when there was no kind of protection for employees, you got laid off and on when bosses wanted to, and I was very much aware of needing to make a living and make ends meet all the time."

Did you have brothers and sisters?

"I've got a twin brother and sister 12 years older than me, then one sister two years older than them."

Did being that many years apart from them have that much effect?

"Yeah, I was born in a different era, as I grew up 12 years on, things like education became far more serious, the government and the country had got their act together post-war, they saw the necessity of a better class of education. I was allowed to further my education beyond 15 which was not normally allowed in my family."

Did you grow up faster?

"Yeah, I was probably more streetwise because I was almost an only kid. Yeah yeah. Happy? Yeah, I suppose so, not unhappy anyway, my parents had done their best to bring us up as best they could. I did enjoy school, got O levels, six or something like that."

You've talked in the past about your father's obsession with money, how he would switch off lights in empty rooms, how there was never enough money. How big an influence was that?

"Everybody wanted more money. My parents never argued about it, just accepted they hadn't got any, they were just ordinary factory workers who had to make ends meet. I suppose from my point of view it was 'how can I get out of this rut in life', it was not what I wanted, having to struggle all the time and worry about where every penny was coming from. That was my objective."

Did you always have a talent for making money?

"Yeah, and a need and a desire to become self-sufficient. If I wanted a bike there was no point in asking dad because he couldn't afford it. I wanted cameras and equipment, so got them myself, did car cleaning and other enterprises."

Did your brother and sisters have the same drive?

"No, I'm not the same as them."

Where did you get it from?

"Dunno, must have been dormant in my mother, or even in father. He was quite intelligent but not a risk taker, very nervous of putting things at risk, also, he was brought up in a war environment and had to worry where every penny was coming from. I know he did have opportunities to start own shop, he was a very good tailor, but at the end of the day the backstop was who is going to pay me on Friday night?."

Anyone else?

"Well, my mother's brother had a shop in Victoria, he was very entrepreneurial, he had a hardware store…"

An assistant passes Sugar a fax. He reads it, betraying no emotion

"Excuse me, I'm trying to do six things at once (studies fax). Yeah, (to assistant) tell Francis that's OK, fax it through. Yeah, my uncle had a hardware store and made a bit of money through the war, investing it in property, he was a bit of an early mentor. I talked to him about the business ideas I had. Yeah, it helped, it showed another side of things. The criteria there was that he was the one in the family that had a car.

So you worked to buy things?

"Yeah, doing it to buy things, to become self-sufficient, and not to have to worry, be self-supporting.

How quickly did you set up on your own?

"Well, having invested in education, I took my first job at the Ministry of Education and Science. I liked science at school, and thought, rather naively, I was going to be involved in all sorts of scientific projects at the ministry, but I ended up with a job in statistics, punching computer cards, very boring. I moved from there to a steel and iron company, their statistics department, and a bunch of chaps there took a liking to me. I was 17. They thought, this chap got's something, and they told me don't waste your time being like we are, just go out and get yourself a job in the commercial world. It's funny how your priorities are when you're young, a set of wheels were the priority for me, so I looked for a job that had a set of wheels. A tape recorder company wanted salesmen to sell tape recorders to shops. I took that."

How did your parents react?

"That was three jobs in a year so my father, who had been in one job for 30 years, was pulling what little amount of hair he had out, he was very concerned and worried that this young fellow was a bit of a renegade."

Did he think you would turn out bad?

"No no no, but he was a worrier, yunno? It wasn't long after that, having been there for a year – I was one of the best salesmen – they refused to give me a rise and I moved on to another company, so that was four jobs! And eventually I came home and said, I'm going to work for myself because the company I was working for, all they were was glorified wholesalers, importers selling to retailers. And that's how I started, I bought some bits and pieces like car aerials, took £100 out of my savings account, bought a mini van for £50 second-hand, spent another £8 on third party insurance and the balance on stock, and in the first week I made £60, buying and selling to shops, that was it, I felt I could do it myself."

What *annoys* me

Did you just have a nous for it?

"Yeah, and a lot of discipline, yunno? A lot of that, you have to discipline yourself when you are working for yourself. There's no-one else to report to on a Monday morning. You have to discipline yourself so by Wednesday you have earned the salary you needed."

Are you good with figures?

"Well, I'm not a brilliant mathematician but quite good with figures, yeah."

A good salesman?

"Very good, yeah, I would say. It's about being logical, yunno, making offers that was difficult for them to refuse, propositions that were no-brainers, make them assume that offers were good, that's always been my forte. Fair value for money, never overselling something, never charging more than you should do. So I set up Amstrad early on in 1968, AMS Trading Co, I had no idea how big it would grow, it was just a company for me to derive a living out of. I don't plan ahead, I just follow the market."

*is **all** this smoke and mirrors stuff*

Do you think luck played a part in your success?

"There's no luck involved in my business success, I've got to tell you that, you can't say it's all luck, always a bit of luck. You can say that in football too but at the end of the season you play 38 games and can't say it was luck that got Manchester United to the championship. I think it is a case of smelling the market, you've got a nose and nous for certain things."

When did you realize you were good at it?

"I never thought I was good at it, it was just organic growth really, as opportunities came along in various sectors and with different products, I sensed those products had a lot of future and jumped into them. The formula was always to manufacture things for a much lower price than others and make things into mass-market products."

Any reason why electronics?

"Electronics is where I started, and as a kid I used to make electronic kits, they always interested me, and I am a bit of a gadget man."

You don't look very enthusiastic about it.

"No, I've got all the latest technology, no question about that."

But you're generally so rude about new technology…

"Well, it's all come true, hasn't it? Everything I said about the net explosion and that rubbish, it annoys me, I mean, I am what I call a fair trader, I believe that the share price in Amstrad or Viglen should go up if doing good business or making profits, that is the old-fashioned way. What annoys me in the last three years is all this smoke and mirrors stuff, people talking about dreams, market totally misunderstanding what was going on. The only people who were making any money out of it were the broker and bankers, and that's it. The poor individual shareholders who got sucked into this nonsense were the ones who lost, it's very frustrating.

Hence the rude articles I've written about these people who haven't got a hope in hell, these dotcom companies, they haven't got a chance of making any money, never will make any money, it's all coming true."

Is that why you moved into property?

"No, there's a break between my personal life and my business. In the public companies I am working on behalf of the shareholders, in my private portfolio for future family planning, property is very boring but a very safe bet. You don't want to have any family wealth tied up in risky things, because we are in the risk business."

Isn't property a risk?

"There are property traders and people who have investment property, and if you buy good-quality investment stuff and buy it for the sake of investment, not highly geared and not borrowing against it, it can survive through the valleys and mountains of recession. That's what's happened to my property stuff, I bought a lot of it 15 odd years ago, it just lay there, it's gone through the valleys and mountains of recession and that hasn't bothered me, it's just sitting there. One thing is for sure, on a long-term basis property will always go up in price, over a 20–30 year period it's going to be a good investment. It's all in planning for the family and the grandchildren and the dynasty…"

Dynasty? (Sugar has two sons and a daughter, all grown up). Isn't there a worry that too much can disincentivize your children?

"Yeah, money could ruin my family but it hasn't because of the way my wife and I have brought our children up, they have always been made to go to work, and to understand, to be realistic in life. They have had a difficult time in having a father like me, of course… but they are not the Ferrari-driving, drug-taking, hippy, yuppy lot, they are ordinary, very good, very nice stable people."

Do you think it is tough following a famous dad?

"Yeah, maybe."

When did you first become well-known?

" Probably when the company floated in 1980."

Have you always had a fair crack from the media?

"I think the financial press, which is more intelligent than the football press, have been very fair, they write it as it is, there's no personal thing, if you're doing well, you're doing well, if you call it wrong, you call it wrong. On balance, I've never had cause to complain about articles written in financial newspapers, though I would like to make that word clear, NEWSPAPERS, because there have been some financial rags that have been a bit stupid."

And the football press?

"Football is completely different, you can't believe a word you read in newspapers, there are so many different agendas, no rhyme or reason."

Has your involvement in football damaged your reputation as a businessman?

"No, I don't think so, in fact, all the football fraternity went on about how I was a good businessman and how I wouldn't allow irresponsible things to happen at a football club, so I don't think so, I think it really homed in on the point."

Any regrets about your time at Tottenham?

"There are a few things that would have been done differently, but I don't want to talk about that now, this interview isn't being given about football. I'm saving that up for another day."

Yet explain this point: financially, you have run the club like any businessman would want to run it. But you were not judged a success. So what was missing?

"Well I should have lied and lied regularly every week about how much money we are going to spend and how we are going to build a big team and how we are going to do this and that, and challenge for things, and not do it, of course, but just kind of like bluff your way through the whole thing as a lot of people do. At the end of the day a lot of hot air is talked by people running football clubs, talking about passion, making sure this happens and that – cheap words, I can't bring myself to say something if not going to do it."

Back to business. What are the mistakes you've made that you've learnt from? Can you, for instance, explain how you lost control of the word processor market in the 80s?

"Looking back, we were very much a small group of people developing products that were a big hit and I don't think… actually, I think we got stuck in a rut doing things in a certain way, we missed the boat in the transition of how to manufacture products, we found ourselves ending up with things a little out of date because of the manufacturing procedure we had, it was very much Far Eastern-oriented, time delays and all that stuff. That's one thing. Then, we exploded the IT market in England and I think we should have invested far more in technical and engineering people to keep us in the forefront, instead of just making products which were very good technologically but transparently easy to use. There was no question that it was a big mistake, but there were also other mistakes which brought us down. In the manufacturing process, the leading-edge technology, as with our disk drives, was quite flakey in those days, the qualification process before they were put into our machines was weak, and the real demise of Amstrad was brought about by the 2000 series where the hard drives didn't work. We took the manufacturers to court and got compensated but that's all after the horse had bolted."

Was it round about then that your problems with the City started?

"People talk about my problems with the City but it was because I wouldn't play their sort of game. (The phone rings) Excuse me. (He takes the call then returns). What was the question? Oh yeah, if you play the public company game properly, you've got 15–20,000 shareholders and they're all entitled to get info at the same time, and a little closed group of preferential shareholders, as they see themselves, should not. And basically I suppose what a lot of people didn't like was the element of surprise – why didn't they know a bit earlier than everyone else about something. And I don't want to play that game. Because I don't think it is fair."

Do you mean brokers and analysts? Can you give a specific instance?

"Well, there were instances when our profits were higher than thought, they would have liked to know, no doubt, so they could have poured in and bought the stock. The first thing they knew was when we announced the results. It's not on, they say, you are supposed to tell us. I've got a lovely anecdote, you know the supposed Chinese wall? 'We'd never tell the other people what's going on'? Well, that's a load of crap, they have done me a couple of times on that in the early days and I got very streetwise on it. We would get a call from the company broker, supposedly on the other side of his Chinese wall, and they would say (posh voice) 'I'm phoning with my corporate advice hat on, how're things going, it's the end of the financial year, are you in line with the forecast we put out? No actually, we've doubled the profits we thought we would make. 'Right, bye, see you!' Phone went down and two hours later the share price starts running away! Now, that's not fair, it's totally unfair. I thought this is not on, this is a group of people who are benefiting for privilege, all this insider-trading stuff, no good anyone else doing it but OK for them. I wouldn't play that game and won't play that game, it goes when there's good news *or* bad news."

Do you think that entrepreneurs always get a rough ride from the stock market?

"I think the point is this, it depends what you want out of life. If you play the game and can be very clever, if you spend most of your time not focusing on the business but meeting them every single day, talking the share price up on a lot of hype and smoke and mirrors... then at the end of the day you can say that's what business is all about, isn't it? I am in the business as the major owner and the share price is going up and actually business is taking second place, but the end-stop is: if I get the share price up that's what the objective is, isn't it? If I can do that by talking it up, why waste my bloody time going out selling products and making profits? We've been through an era recently where lots of people have done that, a lot of people have spent time in corporate soirees, yunno, talking all the time, getting friendly with the press, talking business stuff and giving some other bloke the job of running the core business. This era we have just been through allowed that to happen. Prior to that, of course, it was money talks, profit talks, recently profits haven't talked, all the other rubbish that talked. I hope it gets back to profits talk."

Because your philosophy is different?

"My philosophy is this: I don't have to have lunches with you all the time because at the end of the day we report twice a year, if we bring in profit and have a good dividend and the earnings per share is good then organically, the share price will rise without any intervention from you. Unfortunately we've gone through an era, especially in technology, where profits got nothing to do with share price rise! All sweet-talking and smoke and mirrors and obscure technology that people say they have got and no-one else... Fortunately after the internet explosion we will get back to the time when you didn't have to have all these meetings, fund managers can look themselves every six months and see where it's all going."

Do you think the City of London has given you a fair crack of the whip?

"I'm not complaining, as an individual I've made a lot of money."

What do you think your reputation is?

"I'm not interested in that."

It was reported that when you approached David Potter at Psion with a deal for him to buy Amstrad in 1996, his advisers dissuaded him because they mistrusted your motives. Do you think that's true?

"Well, they were wrong, weren't they? He was going to buy Amstrad for £250m. Well, here's where he should have sued his advisers. £250m – there was already £170m of cash in the business, another business called Dancall which I eventually sold for £90m, then the Seagate litigation (over the supply of faulty hard drives) which hauled in another £80m, so badly advised, very, very badly advised. Well, that's his loss, not mine. He would have laid out 200 million odd quid and accumulated 300-odd million and looked a hero, wouldn't he? He should have sued them."

because **someone**

name doesn't mean they

Are you angry the deal fell through?

"If I'd sold it, people would have said to me, you sold it too cheap. The deal was, I was going to take a load of Psion shares and they rose to dizzy heights."

Would you have sold?

"Most probably, yeah. I mean he sold £100m worth of shares right at the peak, didn't he? Correct me if I'm wrong but the company is not worth two bob at the moment. What's this Symbian thing? All his partners are pulling out, what is this stuff? What's so special about it, I don't think anybody understands it at all."

You sound cross with Dr Potter? Surely it was a long time ago.

"I'm not cross with him, I have been critical but not for printing, he is a…"

Do you think people are more impressed with his insights because he is an academic, and you're not?

*has **titles** after their are the **brightest***

"I don't know if he is…"

Yes, he is.

"Actually my full title is Dr Sugar, you know?"

You're joking.

"No. Doctor of science, yunno? I'm as much of an academic as him, got it somewhere back in 1980-somewhere or other. Remember, I came from a working class background, I could have gone on to university if I had wanted to, but I wanted to earn money. Just because someone has a few titles after their name doesn't mean they are the brightest people going."

Do you always make money out of everything you go into? Even football?

"Yeah, made lots of money out of Tottenham but not for publishing as it will alienate people, but the facts are there."

Did you buy in because of the satellite dish link? Or were you a mole sent in by Rupert Murdoch to influence the TV rights negotiations for soccer?

"Nah, absolute rubbish, I would like from a business ego point of view to say how clever I am but nothing to do with that. Comes a time in life when you've made it, get to 40-odd, got plenty of money, you think, I personally would like to give something back to the community. A lot of community stuff I do I don't make a fuss about. I have built schools and old age homes and supported Great Ormond St Hospital, and Tottenham was really saving my old club, the club I was brought up with"

You didn't buy in for sentimental reasons after your Dad died?

"Not really, but it was our club. Like saving the Hackney Empire, did you see that last week? That's what people do at my age when they realize that the hustling in life is not everything, you give something back, and I like to give something back, yunno? That's why I do these tours talking to young kids."

How come you were a big supporter of Margaret Thatcher and John Major, and then shifted to support Tony Blair?

"Well, old Labour was old Labour and I never liked what it stood for."

Wasn't your father a Labour supporter?

"Yeah, my dad was a Labour supporter but he would have been, wouldn't he?"

Were you rebelling against what he believed in?

"Nah, nothing to do with rebelling against him, nothing like that, got the wrong end of the stick. He was a worker and wanted to be protected and quite rightly so. During certain eras of Labour government… protection of employees was brought in, some may argue that they have gone over the bloody top, human rights and things, fact you can't get rid of someone is ridiculous. But in his day it was totally ridiculous, where you could literally be told on Friday no work, clear off, no compensation, nothing, then it was right to support the Labour Party in those days, right to be a socialist, you can't treat people in that manner. But they went over the top, people like Scargill and all that lot, the strikes and things, that's what drove me against them, you see? Pushed me into the Thatcher way of thinking. She was very good ,she was business-like, she didn't want all these fat companies sitting round poncing off the government so she privatized them all, make them stand up and be counted. Go to British Telecom and say, you can't have this fat existence, charging people what you fancy, have big fat entities and stick it on the consumer, no, you are not going to be alone any more, the railways and everything else, and good luck to her, I agreed with those policies."

And the switch to Blair?

"Then along came Blair, very refreshing attitude, because within the Thatcher days it was still very much an elitest thing, privatize all these things but still 'them and us', City still pinstriped lads who started out in Oxford and all that, shouldn't have any chaps from Hackney in a merchant bank, yunno, you keep your distance, you carry on being the second-hand motor dealers and us lot from Eton and Cambridge will be the elite. Whereas Blair policy is, we're all the same, believe in enterprise, not old Labour, not old Scargill lot, the difference between us and the other lot is the Alan Sugars of this world can run public companies, can trade currencies in the stock market and run a business and can be an MP and can be someone, doesn't have to be some viscount, and that's the attraction. Worst thing about the current government is the name they are lumbered with. New generations won't remember it but it's why they had to use New Labour."

And the speaking tour?

"Personally you get to the stage where you have to contribute something back to society and give up time. Personal not religious, don't like seeing underprivileged people, want to see people from a background like me get an equal chance. Anybody, anybody, literally anybody from any walk of life can do what they like so long as they are honest and straightforward and businesslike, I like to encourage it."

Are we good at producing entrepreneurs in this country?

"Definitely there is interest in entrepreneurial activity, we are good at it but have to recognize who is good at it and who isn't and sort out those who really are from the ones that say they are. It is in-built in you, like a musician's or artist's talent. You can't go into WH Smith and buy a book and become an entrepreneur. You have got to have some killer instinct in you. We can't all be entrepreneurs, we can't all be Richard Bransons, we can't all be Anita Roddicks, we can't all be them. There are some that have a way of exploiting things, understanding things quickly, accepting things quickly and others that can't do it. A word that is used too frequently by people, shouldn't be allowed to use it, should be illegal to let someone call themselves entrepreneur. I can't call myself a doctor or a lawyer because I don't have the qualifications."

I thought you just said you were a doctor. I've got you, I think...

"No, no, not a medical doctor. Got me? No you haven't, I can do anything else other than hysterectomies."

And entrepreneurs?

"It's the way you are born, what's in you, brain power, fast brain, aptitude for the business you are in, quick understanding of what can be done and what can't be done, watching the way markets change, jumping in quickly and exploiting them, and having the sense of what the end-user wants."

Do you think you've mellowed?

"Yes, definitely, no question of it, but you do with age, I understand why some successful companies have 58-year-old chairmen, you're not there to do business but because you've been there and done it and worn the T-shirt and can reflect, and say, look youngsters, before you rush in, I have been there blah blah, and on a positive front you can look at an opportunity whereas others might miss it."

Do you have regrets about your personal style? You are well-known for being aggressive, the grudges, the swearing....

"I do use a lot of rude words but horses for courses – fortunately in my life I have been invited to dine with the past three prime ministers and been out to dinner with His Royal Highness the Prince of Wales, and the greatest moment I suppose was when I was invited to lunch with the Queen, and it wouldn't have gone down too well if I had gone in f'ing and blinding there, would it? Even though one of her corgis was piddling on my ankle at the time."

Really?

"Well, it tried to, didn't it? But you have to adapt to company you are in. I can have a good old swear-up in the right company, but I never swear in front of women and children. Generally I adapt to the company I am in, when in Rome, so to speak. I am never going to change, if you don't like it, keep away from me. Simple as that. I am not looking for friends or fans really."

How do you divide your time between work and relaxation? Do you still have the large boat in the Med?

"No, I sold my boat. I've got homes in Florida and Spain and England, I do property development, I got Amstrad and Learning Technology to run."

Do you still play a lot of tennis?

"Yes."

Are you good?

"Reasonably good club standard."

Do you beat Malcolm Miller (Sugar's old number two, now chief executive of rival Pace, and another tennis nut)?

"Easily, no questions, beat him reading the Financial Times in between rallies! No, he's too heavy. Some of the pictures I have seen of him lately, he should cut down on the saltbeef sandwiches, you tell him from me. No, he's a good old bloke, Malcolm, there's no animosity between us."

And on a Sunday?

"I sit around and relax, watch TV, play football in the field with my grandchildren."

Are you any good?

"I am no good at all, and no, I never get famous footballers round."

How do you spend your money?

"Not on pictures or books, I'm not big on that kind of stuff, got all these homes, they cost money to run. I've got an aeroplane, that's my luxury."

Staff?

"Not a lot, really. I've got a good lifestyle, not stingy in any way or form, I don't begrudge myself any of that, I've worked hard for it, I didn't rob any banks and I'm not a drug dealer, I am entitled to do it."

Are you a godfather figure to the rest of the Sugar family now, to your brother and sisters?

"Nah, I am the baby of the family. They don't work for me but we're very close."

Do you ever go back to Hackney?

"No, but a lot of my friends are ordinary working class people, I've got four or five friends who meet regularly who I knew at 17, they don't live in Hackney now, they're in all walks of life."

Do they tell you what footballers to buy?

"No, they don't."

One last thing, was it you that said, 'I don't know what's worse, £20m in the hands of a marketing man or in the hands of a football coach'?

"Yeah, that's my words."

I like that.

"Good."

Kalms describes

"*one of the* *great*

He growls and jumps

And with that we parted, Sugar walking off to have his photograph taken, never smiling, never, seemingly, that interested in what we were talking about, apart from the moment when he vented his spleen on David Potter. The claim to be a doctor of science is, I think, a joke. I may be wrong. With a man who never smiles or laughs, it's hard to tell.

And those grudges. Why can't he let them go? When I relay the conversation to Sir Stanley Kalms, chairman of Dixons stores and an old sparring partner of Sugar's, he laughs and says, oh, Alan's just feeding you. "You're a journalist, you need to be fed, it gives you three paragraphs for your piece."

And, adds Kalms, what people don't realize about Sugar is that a lot of it *is* an act, he is the ultimate, straight-faced comedian. "He growls and jumps and likes to provoke and irritate but he is 100% focused on what he wants

Sugar as
entrepreneurs
of our era"

to achieve." Kalms, who describes Sugar as "one of the great entrepreneurs of our era", says he has been offended in the past by his aggression, particularly his habit of writing long, vituperative letters. "But then you ring Alan the next day and it's 'Hi Stanley, how're ya doin'!' and you realize he's forgotten, he just had to get it off his chest."

Another close to Sugar is not so sure. He says that it's all part of the man's make-up: he hates "bullshit", always wants to avenge a slight, and only trusts those who have come the same way as him, with the same values. Hence the preponderance of men from north and east London, unaffluent backgrounds, second or third-generation immigrant, who have formed his executive cadre: Malcolm Miller, former Amstrad md, now chief executive of Pace Micro (16-year stint), Bordan Tkachuk, another ex-Amstrad md, now ceo of Viglen (13-year stint). All have the same attributes – good at numbers, quick to gross and net.

The style is aggressively
are commonplace
over-promised:

"If you look at the commercial people around Alan, we can all trade, do a deal and make it stick," says Tkachuk, adding that what Sugar respects is people who stand up to him. The style is aggressively macho, nicknames are commonplace (the salesman who over-promised: Goldenbollocks), he is tough on employees who fail, he does demand constant access to his executives – "when he rings he expects to talk to you" – and he always cuts through any waffle.

Some, like me, are rather intimidated by this front, especially his refusal to exchange even the smallest of pleasantries before getting down to business. Why doesn't he make the effort? "Because he doesn't have to," shrugs Tkachuk. Does *he* think Sugar has mellowed? "I haven't noticed it," laughs Tkachuk.

A lot of that makes Sugar rather unsuited to certain kinds of business, especially those where emollience and PR assume any importance. Hence his problems running a football club. Tottenham fans hated him simply for

macho, nicknames
(the salesman who
Goldenbollocks)

not promising the earth. Hence his jibe about "should have lied every week".

And some of what he says just isn't logical, especially when he's waging his own private class war. Men from Hackney not being allowed to run public companies in the 80s? That's when he floated his company, for goodness' sake! That's when the dealing rooms of every broker in the City were flooded with non-Oxbridge, non-public-school men working their way to the top through ability, not connections. It's just not consistent – a bit, perhaps, like Sugar's support of whichever prime minister is in power. Not consistent, but opportunistic.

Which is his key trait, and his weakness. Why did he never make the final leap to building a really big multinational company? He had the chance with Amstrad word processors – he had a global market in his hands, and he let it slip. He was sabotaged by the faulty hard drives on a new line but it was more than that. "Some of it must be people," says one who's worked

Could he have been *without* the

with him. "More of the companies could have moved out internationally. Something went wrong." Another in the electronics business suggests that, as Sugar is a hands-on boss, expecting him to build a huge multinational is unrealistic. "Alan can't delegate," he chuckles. "The limit of his powers are in the scope of his personal control."

Sugar admits, he ballsed up. But it's happened again and again. Why did Amstrad let Pace barge into its market for set-top boxes? Why does Sugar never learn? "Because Alan's strategy is based on blockbuster success," says one former Amstrad man. "Put out ten products and if one is a hit it doesn't matter about the other nine." Too many corners cut, too much leaping around, too little focus – too opportunistic.

And why does he have to be so tough? One rival suggests that, despite all the success, Sugar still has a nagging inferiority complex. "That's why he behaves so aggressively. He's frightened to have an intellectual conversation but because of his powers of insight he will come to a conclusion, and give

even more successful
fuck-you
aggression?

it to you right between the eyes." The strange thing is, he is right most of the time. "Most people would rationalize it for you, with Alan it's bang, bang."

And remember, says the same source, Sugar has had a rough time from the press for years, they have been very critical of his business style. Only two months before I had met him, he had won a libel case against the *Daily Mail* when they accused him of being a miserly football chairman, with all those horrible, old, anti-Jewish connotations. He's bound to keep the defences up, even though he is trying to rebuild his standing after the torrid time at Tottenham. Only his old mates, many of whom he's known since his Hackney days, see the true Sugar. "He is surrounded by a small coterie of very loyal friends into whom he nestles and is an entirely different person. He has kept his friends from days of yore and when he moves out, he faces an aggressive world." Hence the act.

The odd thing is, he doesn't even let it drop for those who work with him. He rarely socializes with his key executives, keeps his home life private, and despite the houses in Essex, Florida and Spain, the blue Rolls-Royce, the private plane, doesn't like people to think he has an extravagant, 'unrealistic' lifestyle, especially with regards to his children, two sons and a daughter, all grown up now. Hence the bristling "not your Ferrari-driving, drug-taking, hippy, yuppy lot".

And that's the only Sugar we are allowed to see. Hard. It's how he describes himself, "not a lovey-dovey person". It's what he's built round himself in his drive to make a fortune, and what he has clearly found to be his greatest asset as it's scared the pants off many of his rivals, and kept a lot of people at a distance who he doesn't want near him. And keeping that up must take discipline. Could he have been even more successful without the fuck-you aggression? Or would that have neutered his drive? We'll never know.

His last words to me, when he left the photo session, were a typically grudging, "You told me it would only be bloody two minutes!" as he stomped off up the stairs. What is wrong with him? I thought. Then just as I was writing him off as a grumpy old bastard, I distinctly heard the hint of a chuckle.

DETOURED BRAINS

You don't have to be an intellectual to start a business, in fact...

THEY USED TO SAY BRAINS WERE A HINDRANCE TO entrepreneurial ambition, don't go to university, get out there while you're young, get experience. Classic entrepreneurs were men like Sir Alan Sugar, who were uncomplicated in their ambitions, didn't need exams to prove themselves, just the right edginess to ride the flow of money in, money out. Too much brains would capsize you, weigh you down like a backpack of heavy books in the current of capitalism. They used to say that.

More on David Potter

I meet Potter, founder of Psion, at a bad time: six months after his heart by-pass operation, one month after he had started work again, weeks from a new product launch. It's the middle of 1997 and all around the giants of the new techno-world, Microsoft, Hewlett-Packard, Sharp, are closing in, looking to squash his little British success story. Walking away from the deal to buy Amstrad is the least of his worries…

Potter, then 53, face as round and brown as a roasted almond, top teeth clamping onto bottom lip, eyes pulled wide as if by the sun, is twitchy. "Only the paranoid survive," he says, declaiming the Silicon Valley motto that had only just gained currency. Then he adds, looking suitably glum, "I profoundly believe that and the worst thing about Bill Gates is that he knows it too."

That's how he talks, an edge of morbid wit just tinging the corner of his words like a dark stain. Back then – he has somewhere grander now, I think – he was sitting in a little office on top of an unimpressive block down a side road off the wrong end of London's Edgware Road. Strange location? He has four or five buildings in the area, he says, because he likes it. It's where he started Psion, it's close enough to his house in St John's Wood and it's cheap. He is probably the only hi-tech multimillionaire boss to have a personal office just a washing line away from a block of council flats, one of which has such a good view into his personal sanctum that you can only presume that its tenant has already sublet it to Seattle. If Potter was really paranoid, he'd move.

But maybe he's moved enough. Potter is South African by birth, British by inclination, an ex-academic, the first of the new wave of phd bosses. He'd shifted from a bit of share dabbling while still teaching to setting up a software house then producing hardware, notably Psion's handheld electronic organizers. He had been making them for over a decade when we met, building a steady customer base, both consumer and business-to-business. What was more remarkable was not that he had had the idea, but that the big companies had left him to it for so long. No-one had taken him seriously. Since when did academics build big companies? Now they had turned round, spotted his market share and gone, who the hell is that? How did he create this market? How can we muscle him out? That is when an entrepreneur faces a true test: how to cling on to what you've got. That's when you learn what, as they used to say, you are made of.

> *Brain: the mass of substance contained in the skull of humans and other vertebrates... The organ of thought, memory or imagination... sing. and (freq.) in pl. a clever person, the cleverest person in a group etc, the mastermind* (OXFORD ENGLISH DICTIONARY)

Kids who need parents are weaklings

Potter is an introspective man – unlike the old breed of entrepreneurs – and enjoys teasing out his own psychology. He describes to me his family tree.

"I was born in South Africa, my parents were South African, I guess I was predominantly third or fourth-generation empire, as far as I know. My great-great-grandparents emanated out of England and Ireland, from Manchester, Royston and County Cork. My maternal grandfather was the son of a printing works manager at a company called Snape in Salford. That grandfather became the youngest chief engineer to London County

Council in 1901, then became an academic and was attracted out to the University of Cape Town to set up a department of engineering. My grandmother's side were grocers out of Burford in the Cotswolds. I have got one sister and two half-brothers. I lost my father when I was very young, he died of cancer when I was a few years old. I have no memories of him, except, I remember his voice vaguely. I read recently that an enormous proportion of chief executives in the FTSE100 have lost their fathers in their early years…"

"My mum was a nurse. I had a strange childhood but a very happy one. Because I didn't have a father, I didn't know what it was to have a father. My mother took the role of father and went off to work and my grandmother played the role of mother. We were fairly on the poorish side.

"Grandfather was still alive, I had a very happy childhood. Looking back, though, I realize various things one did for not having a father. My sister and I were very close; when we swam in galas we didn't have others to watch us, my mother was busy, so we developed a culture in which kids who needed parents to watch them were seen as weaklings and pathetic."

And business? What drew him into that?

"I think," he says, "my grandfather was an influence. All of us are different but in my particular case it was a mix of academic and intelligence on one hand and practical and business on the other. If you had asked me at 10 or 12, I would have seen myself eventually as being in business, or maybe an engineer… One consequence of not having a father and having an enormous amount of freedom as a child, also the nature of my grandmother and mother, was that I had a lot of confidence and self-reliance, I was super-confident, perhaps a bit thick in some ways. There was that element. Then coming through in the 60s as a student, it was a very confident time, there was the Beatles, the 'white heat of technology', it was natural to do a doctorate, writing papers and books and then get

I read that an enormous
chief executives
lost
in their early years...

tenure, it was fun, I just got involved and never intended to spend the rest of my life in academe, but being a doctoral student is terrific fun."

But why end up running a technology business? He shrugs.

"I am a person who is interested in how the world evolved, in innovation. If I was around in 1948 maybe I would have been interested in biochemistry, I'm thinking of Crick now, who was a physicist, got caught up in the war and decided to study biology and was glad he did. There is a time and place for everything... If I was in the nineteenth century I would have been happy building a bridge over the Firth of Forth. In the 1910s or 1920s I would have been a physicist, as there was a great flowering of ideas then, or to have been in the car industry, that would have been terrific fun, it is always fun to participate in a great movement of ideas and industry."

So when the new technological age blossomed, when e-world beckoned, Potter could not resist. Why has he been successful – just brains? No, he laughs, it's chutzpah, risk-taking, making the leap.

proportion of
in the FTSE100 have

their fathers

"I have been very lucky, and a bit foolhardy. I had a lot of self-confidence, which allowed me to find the opportunity. You know, I have seen a lot of people who through caution or not having the sense of opportunity, get stuck in nooks which are not very exciting where they don't lead very exciting lives as a result. And I do feel in Britain we are living in a very cautious era for young people, they are much too cautious. Whoever thought of selling pensions to young people?"

Does being born outside Britain help? Is an immigrant less cautious?

"Yah," he says, with faint South African intonation. "I think so, almost by definition. You tend to be less cautious and more open if you go somewhere else."

Really? Those foreign roots have given him a useful half-in, half-out perspective on what goes on here – they make him reluctant to accept the status quo, make him think more things are possible, less likely to worry about what others say or think. Maybe that goes with the academic background too, and the technology he works with: new ways of doing business, new insights, new areas.

Interruption from a technology guru

Kevin Kelly, prophet for the network economy, former executive editor of *Wired* magazine, has seen the future of business. He has spent ten years rehearsing it. Read his books *Out of Control* and *New Rules For The New Economy*. He predicts a future where relationships with customers become even more valuable, where intangibles like trust and human attention will have huge value, where the whole structure of corporate hierarchies will change. Government and business pay him large sums to explain his vision.

I buy him dinner in a Copenhagen restaurant, after he'd spent a long day giving a lecture seminar to Scandinavian corporates followed by assorted press interviews. He's knackered, pale and pasty, nearly 50, with sad eyes, thinning hair and a tentative smile. His manner is kind and courteous. He eats while fending off another barrage of questions from me. One answer he gave sticks in the mind. When I ask him whether the psychology of those who set up and run successful businesses will change, he thinks about it a bit, and says, no, essentially not, then mulls it over, pondering aloud while he chews.

"The thing about business," he says, "is that there are such an incredible variety of people working in it, and they all have their own stories. Will the psychology of people who are successful change? No, I don't think it will. But maybe I should rethink that. There are many roads to prosperity and success, and I am not of the opinion that success demands a certain psychology. Most successful businesses are projections of personality, and, in my view, the most successful businesses are the most successful projections, and there's really no limit. It's just about opening up the possibilities and shapes. There will always be big companies like Procter & Gamble and Unilever, there will still be authoritarian businesses, mom and pop businesses, Jack Welch-type businesses, whatever kind. But out here" – he gestures with his fork, jabbing it to the left – "there will be all kinds of other businesses that have never existed before, all kinds of other personalities who have never before had a business..."

Riding the front of the wave

How does a former academic like Potter run his company? With the emphasis on innovation. He used to attribute his success to "Riding the Front of the Wave", a phrase he liked so much that he gave it capital letters and put it on the front of one of his annual reports. He also likes to remind people that the company is here for the long haul, repeatedly telling journalists he's a "long-distance runner". The market valuation of Psion may swing wildly depending on whether tech is in or out of fashion, but the core values will keep it pushing through.

He explains: "What Psion does is not just make palm-top computers or just be Europe's number one company in portable data communication. What we do is innovation and development. And we are always moving on, that's why we talk about riding the front of the wave. We are always moving on, pursuing high added value with high-margin products and markets. That's why we don't produce low-end calculators, we produce leading-edge palm-top computers. We don't produce low-end fax machines, we produce GSM data cards. It's a business philosophy built around innovation and creating added value which you can exploit in this particular industry."

He describes his style of management as "collegiate". Many of the team have been with him from the early days, and he is intensely loyal to them. Everyone is drawn into product development, even the non-executive directors, at the earliest stage. Everything is discussed.

Danny Fiszman, diamond dealer and majority shareholder in Arsenal football club, put a large stake into Psion a decade ago and is now a non-executive director. He says it is an extraordinarily close-knit team, which hinges around Potter, but it isn't, as many people think, a one-man band. "It's just that David is good at everything: understanding the market place, running the balance sheet. He's that rare animal, both academic and commercially minded."

But since when have academics made good company bosses? Potter says it's not brains but chutzpah that counts. That's why he came over from South Africa when offered a scholarship to Trinity College, Cambridge to read natural sciences. He stayed, married a journalist, got his phd from Imperial College in London, did a stint on sabbatical at UCLA in California, and returned to a post at Imperial, where he published an important text on computational physics. He says he had always been interested in business but those who studied under him at Imperial say his American experience was formative: in California, the path between academia and Mammon was well worn. Others suggest the wide circle of friends that he made through his wife, who was one of the Insight team which worked on

he decided
going to be

the Thalidomide story at *The Sunday Times*, was also a factor in his decision to look for other opportunities.

It was while he was in America that he started investing, putting all his savings into British blue chip companies at the bottom of the 1974 bear market, and then, as the market recovered, shifting his profits into little niche companies he had winkled out. All he was doing, he says, was applying his academic training to the markets, properly researching prospective investment targets. But he had the trademark Potter confidence, too. When, for instance, he decided duvets were going to be the next big thing, he tracked down a manufacturer in Lincolnshire and simply rang the chairman up.

"I said 'my name is David Potter, I am a potential investor and I would like to come and interview you'. And he said fine. It was probably the first time any investor or analyst had shown any interest. Actually, I think the chutzpah I had was unbearable." But people today, he sighs, especially young people, are just so *cautious*. Of course, in-depth research for relatively

duvets were
the next
big thing

small investments hardly sounds reckless, and those who have worked closely with Potter over the years say that in fact he is actually the most financially conservative of anyone at Psion, though that, laughs one of his executives, might have something to do with the large personal stake he still has in his company. So how does one square that circle: risk and caution? It's called judgement...

Potter started Psion in 1980, using the money he made on the markets. Initially he published software for microcomputers, picking up other people's work, packaging and marketing it. A year later, with the profits from that, he set up his own software development team, luring in one of his old students from Imperial, Charles Davies, to head it up. Davies remembers it as a one man and a dog operation. "And I was the dog," he says. But the software sold and a year later Potter brought in Andy Clegg, an ex-British Aerospace design engineer, and set both of them to work on an idea for a simple, hand-held computer.

Psion launched its first Organiser in 1984, and built sales steadily, especially in the corporate market. Key contracts like that with Marks & Spencer, which initially gave the machines to staff to check credit cards, ensured credibility. The usual problems that hit successful small companies – soaring administration costs, cash flow hiccups, difficulties in foreign markets, getting the right new investors in – were overcome. In 1986 Psion launched the Organiser II. In 1988 it became a public company. In 1991 it launched its Series 3 range of palm-top computers. By this stage Potter's little machines were combining electronic diary, address book and alarm clock functions with powerful word processing and spreadsheet capabilities. And they were selling to consumers as fast as to corporate clients. An upgraded Series 3a and industrial Workabout range followed.

And Psion grew and grew. In 1996 Potter reorganized into four separate companies: computers, software, enterprise and data communications – a decision he later described as one of the best but most difficult business moves he had made. The software side became independent in order to license software more widely, and in turn became a new joint venture, Symbion, formed with Ericsson, Nokia and Motorola, to develop wireless software for mobile phones. That has long been tipped for a separate float, although tensions between the founders may scupper that deal. Then there was the Amstrad opportunity. Potter pulled out of that, a move which, of course, earned him the undying enmity of Sir Alan Sugar. Sugar wastes no time in telling people now that he thinks technologists like Potter have taken the market for a ride. Potter, when I met him, said he rather liked Sugar.

And mistakes? They take years to filter through the system. What seems obvious becomes insane. Potter cites not buying American rival Palm in 1995 when it ran out of money. He was, he says, approached by the founders but baulked at the offer price of $30m. They didn't show me what the software could do, he complained later.

Recently Potter has stepped back from day-to-day control, handing over to a chief executive, probably more for health reasons than any other. Investors want to make sure that the company is not too much of a one-man band. The new chief executive has sold off one of Psion's manufacturing sites, staff numbers have been reduced, the emphasis moved from hardware to software. But Potter has always argued that the values must stay the same; he knows where entrepreneurs trip up, he has rationalized it all.

"It is important to understand what has been successful in the past. The question is how you get other managers to employ new people in Psion who will reproduce the DNA, if you like, which has been successful in the past. I am a builder not a shrinker. I have been through difficult times, ups and downs, and no doubt go through more in the future, but a good manager has to manage through those circumstances, nothing goes in a straight line. I think I am a realist. What is true is that I am very financially aware. I am very cost-conscious. A lot of people… I've seen them come and go, it really is interesting how many companies come and go, people with great ideas that don't stay the course. In ten years' time, provided the DNA goes the right way, I should be able to design and develop this enterprise on a larger scale and hopefully on an enduring scale. But patience is important."

How big?

"You need to be an appropriate size for the markets you are addressing. I have never believed there will be just one company which will end up ruling the world – I might be wrong, it might be Bill Gates – but there were articles professing that in 1956 and it's not true. One of the great things about capitalism is that successful organizations become smug and fat and get pulled down. So you get big companies downsizing and new companies from below generating new employment. It's a virtuous circle. Thank God for that or we would all be ruled by a bunch of pompous old…"

Bit reckless

But you've got to be a bit reckless, a bit bold. Brains are not enough without that appetite for risk. Maybe brains make most people too cautious. Not everyone, though. Brent Hoberman, founder of lastminute.com, wrote his initial business plan with his best friend, Rogan Angelini-Hurll. They had been at Eton and Oxford together. Hoberman describes Angelini-Hurll as the brightest guy he has ever worked with. Angelini-Hurll, who works as a research analyst at Salomons, describes Hoberman as driven, obsessional and a winner. Yet when the time came to chuck in what they were doing and start the business, Angelini-Hurll stalled.

"I've got a theory," he told me, "that those entrepreneurs that succeed are the ones with either no money and nothing to lose or quite a bit of money. Brent had quite a bit of money. I had a good job, a wife, a baby. I had too much to lose."

Hoberman now has even more money, possibly, since lastminute got up and running.

The brain is a wonderful organ

It starts working the moment you get up in the morning, and does not stop until you get into the office (Robert Frost)

Normally

"I was blessed with this wonderful quality called the naivety of youth."

Dr Mike Lynch laughs with a throaty chuckle, part nervous, part infectious. He is still getting used to people wanting a part of him, digging into his motivations, quizzing him about his private life, commenting on his clothes and his baldness and his beard. That leap to business celebrity is the toughest challenge for academic entrepreneurs. They, more than any, see so little purpose in it all.

Short, squat, slightly paunchy with Slavic eyes, Lynch looks uncomfortable in any interview. You can tell he would rather quiz than be quizzed. He has an ungiving face, suspicious, slightly menacing when his left eyebrow rises. Much of the time he scowls, and looks unnervingly like Lenin – a resemblance which perhaps persuaded him to remove his beard before floating his company Autonomy on the UK stock market in 1999. By that time, as a man holding a paper value of many millions if not billions of pounds (Autonomy was already listed on Easdaq and Nasdaq), he was entitled to do what he wanted with his facial hair.

And his business and academic lives are enmeshed like a plaited weave. Lynch studied mathematics at Cambridge, read for a phd, and evolved his research around the probability theories of the great Rev Thomas Bayes, eighteenth century cleric and mathematician, into groundbreaking computer software that could provide pattern-recognition tools for

Mike Lynch

everyone from the police force (fingerprints) to just about everybody putting up search packages on the net. In other words, his software enables others to go about the front-end internet stuff, which is why Lynch's favourite analogy for his business is to describe it as "selling shovels to the people digging" in the Gold Rush. It is an analogy that others have been swift to use for their businesses too: look, it says, low-risk, split options, back us.

That, say advisers, is what Lynch is really good at, communicating simply – as well as raking in cash and holding onto his own. He could have sold out to bigger players many times in his short business life but he never has, he always wanted to run his own operation(s) himself.

"Mike is just incredibly commercial," one of his investors told me. "When we started negotiating with him, he was a 27-year-old academic. But it was like dealing with a 45-year-old serial entrepreneur. He's extraordinary." He rationalizes, he acts, he progresses but if he is a complex person, it rarely shows. "Mike is just very straightforward," says one of his executives. "He says what he thinks without worrying about it."

When I ask Lynch who had most influence on his short business career, he replies promptly "John Harrison". No, not a recent management guru, but the eighteenth century clockmaker who fought convention and snobbery (from posh astronomers) to invent a workable theory of longitude. Lynch looks rather disappointed when I say, yes, of course. It made me think that maybe Lynch, from a less affluent background than many who attend Cambridge University, was already mythologizing his own success. One against the many, a pioneer surrounded by unsympathetic spectators, the razor-sharp oik slicing up the toffs.

But he says it is about challenging preconceptions. He applies those same views through to company management and recruitment. "Things are changing in business on an amazing time scale and it's not predictable any more, so you need people who realize there are not rules about what happens next." That is why, in running his companies, he has learnt to love "outsiders", executives from other cultures who have experience of other worlds and other industries. "I love having mixtures," he says, "that's where you get real benefit."

But it is clearly a mixing of elites. When we met in 1999, Lynch was running three companies with close to 200 employees: Neurodynamics (his first), Autonomy (his biggest) and NCorp (a relatively new e-commerce venture). Autonomy, based outside Cambridge, has a reputation for hiring only the fiercely bright. "They have to be," agrees Lynch, "because the composition we have requires more per employee, it's a big-turnover company with a small amount of people – what we are not doing is process-based management, which is what all other businesses do."

Lynch describes the open plan offices as a "very fast, quite blunt, incredibly young environment". Everyone mixes together, marketing next to research, anyone can bring their dog in (Lynch has a huge otter hound which, he says, is so laid back "he's like a hippy who's been smoking pot all day"). The atmosphere, say others, is democratic and vibrant, Lynch often to be found huddling between the desks of his research crew, whiteboarding out ideas algorithmically. Staff turnover, says Lynch proudly, is almost zero for those who last the first three months.

He is clearly in love with the Cambridge base – one of the reasons he has never emigrated to America, as many expected him to once Autonomy took off (over half Autonomy's revenues come from the US). He keeps an office in the company's American HQ in San Francisco, works there two weeks in four and has an American girlfriend. But he says he had to have an American base because the market and the money is there, and he is suprisingly caustic in his views on Silicon Valley culture.

"Silicon Valley is completely and utterly self-referential, everyone does everything by proxy. You could turn up with a working time machine and be ignored unless you have got the right person on board."

The worst part, he says, was how in the early days, he couldn't get anyone even to speak to him at social events. "I would talk to someone and the guy would just walk away. The sad thing is they are really missing a trick, they really need to have conversations with the odd guy in the corner because that's where the deals are. Now we are the people everyone wants to talk to, and it just makes us cynical."

So cynical, he says, that he and his team have invented a game for Silicon Valley parties, whereby one of them gets nominated to spread a rumour about an amazing, fictional start-up, and they wait to see how long it takes for the rumour to come back to them in the cocktail chatter. "And you know what?" asks Lynch. "It always happens by the end of the evening."

You've got to move

Lynch's mouth moves faster than his dark eyes.

Close-up: "I was born in Ilford but I left it rapidly – haha – my father is a fireman, my mother a nurse, I grew up in Chelmsford, Essex. What was it like? Actually, it is quite difficult to judge Chelmsford till you move away…"

Mike Lynch's epiphany

But why not mainstream business? Not for him, he says. He became badly disillusioned after a holiday stint with GEC Marconi in Chelmsford. He is withering in his contempt for the company. "I got their 'get up and go' culture – basically anyone with 'get up and go' had got up and gone! It was like a cliché, the offices looked like rubbish, the equipment wasn't there, everyone was waiting for some poor guy to die so they could move up a chair…"

everyone was waiting for
so they

This was the company, he adds, which used to turn up at British universities and show glossy videos of fighter planes and cream off the brightest people. "And it was all cost-accounting driven, which is the big British problem. I came back from that and thought, there is no way I am going to do that for the rest of my life."

For what Lynch wants, like many academic entrepreneurs, is the challenge of complexity, the buzz of overcoming the seemingly insurmountable, staying top of the class in a school where he writes the rules too. He even, whispers one of his advisers to me, likes to fill in his own tax form, he just loves the perplexity and the possibilities. Imagine that? And when he is not on the office whiteboard or stuck on a jet mid-Atlantic, he likes to tinker, to pull apart and rebuild old machinery bought from agricultural fairs near his Suffolk home. There is even a miniature steam engine and railway line which he has set out around his garden like an Edwardian industrialist. "I like old things," he says, "you can learn from them. People always seem to think that we are cleverer than our ancestors but it's just not true."

some poor guy to die
could
move up a chair

So he collects "old rubbish" and he also collects time. "I like doing that. You are only gone an hour in my business and everything is changing. It takes me an hour to drive into work, through winding country lanes with no traffic, and I see the seasons change…"

Time is what he doesn't have enough of, he says, but time is what he, more than most, has whittled away with his innovations that speed up computer traffic. A noose for his own neck, as it were.

The funny thing about academic entrepreneurs...

…says a ceo I know, is that once they start complaining about their share price, and how little others understand their business, and how badly rated their company is, as soon as they hit adversity and start hinting at the smallest tad of intellectual arrogance, touching on the raw nerve that says they're so much brighter than the rest of us, their shares tumble twice as fast as everyone else's. It's as if the market is saying: they're not really as smart as they think they are. That'll show 'em.

Money

By the spring of 2001 both Potter and Lynch had come in for severe criticism for cashing in shares shortly before their companies fell steeply in value. Both had made millions of pounds off the (over)rating of their companies. Both had watched, bolstered by their cash piles, as the value of their companies sank. Lynch complained vociferously that analysts and investors didn't understand what was going on. The shares fell faster.

Were people more disappointed because it was them? Do they care any less about what others think and say? Should they have clung on to all their shares and ridden the same rollercoaster as their investors for the sake of propriety?

Would you?

SLY AMBITION

booster rocket

AMBITION IS ADMIRED AND MISTRUSTED. IT CARRIES WITH IT intimations of drive and unpleasantness, focus and vainglory. The smart cover their steps. The over-confident don't care. The young cling on to it like a booster rocket.

> *Ambition: an ardent desire for distinction. Ostentatious display, pomp, an instance of this. Personal solicitation of honours. An aspiration to be, to do. An object of ardent desire or aspiration.*
>
> (OXFORD ENGLISH DICTIONARY)

Talent spotting

The first I heard about Charlie Hoult was when he e-mailed me – typical Charlie, said his friends, always hassling for attention. Hoult, PR man turned entrepreneur, wanted me to look at his latest project, an e-business incubator called metrocube based in an old building on the river in the City of London, bang next door to the Millennium Bridge.

Hoult's scheme was simple: take a short-term lease, wire up the premises, give it a lick of paint, call it an incubator, charge £500 a desk per month, sell a few services, throw a party every so often and don't pressurize the occupants for equity in their businesses. He already ran a successful tech PR agency, Wilson Harvey, out of the building, and funded the expansion from the proceeds of some technology newsletters he had just sold, and backing from well-heeled investors, including his father, the deputy Lord Lieutenant of Tyne and Wear.

Slim, medium-height, dressed in smart trousers and an open-necked shirt – no T-shirts here – Hoult, 33, showed me round while I pondered whether this wasn't more office rental than incubation. Previous versions of the incubator concept, imported from America, involved taking stakes in the businesses, handholding the young entrepreneurs through the money-raising, offering experience and know-how. At one time they were ten a penny in London and outside, all with loud PR and suitably trendy names – Antfactory, Brainspark, E-start, Oxygen. Recently it seemed to have gone quiet.

Yet despite uncertainty in e-world (stocks crashing, big-name firms going to the wall) Hoult's building was full. Six months after opening he was already planning to open another, off Finsbury Circus near Moorgate, to cope with the extra demand, with promises of more to come. London's little e-business start-ups seemed to like his approach. He talked about setting up metrocubes in different cities, in different countries. Others believed in his concept, not least Luke Johnson, who when not chairing Belgo also backed an incubator fund, New Media Spark. Johnson, who fancies himself as an early spotter of promising talent, had put a six-figure sum behind Hoult.

By the time I met Hoult, it looked like Johnson's judgement was paying off. The DTI had offered metrocube and Wilson Harvey, plus three other

what struck me a

was how

partners, a £1.4m contract to launch a portal promoting internet mentoring and incubation in the regions. The deal was a pretty useful chunk of anyone's money, not least taxpayers', especially as the plus-point for those involved was that, if the project works, the partners would have access to a string of new start-ups coming through.

But what struck me at that first meeting was how sly ambition now has to be. Despite inviting me in, despite asking for the publicity, Hoult's approach once I was there was positively diffident. "Oh yeah," he says, "I did win an award, I think it was a Top 5 Entrepreneur of the Year award from *Enterprise* magazine, probably only five people entered." He laughed. Don't be fooled. Someone sent in that entry form, and you can bet it was Hoult himself.

I wondered whether he had thought all this out. Hoult, former public schoolboy and one-time nightclub runner, was so low-key and self-deprecating that it was rather engaging. He told me I would be better off writing about his sister Anabel, another metrocube backer, who had helped

that meeting
sly *ambition*
now has to be

run his newsletters and now headed Carphone Warehouse's European e-commerce arm. But hadn't he suggested I write about him? No, no, just his business ideas. Later he told me that Johnson had advised him to put someone else in to run metrocube – he'd installed an old friend, Rob Kelsey – because keeping out of the headlines reduced the pressure. Really? At the same time his sister told me pointedly that because Charlie had trained as a journalist, he knew what journalists wanted to hear. "That's something that other entrepreneurs don't have a fix on," she said.

Yet to me, if nothing else, his connections *were* intriguing. Metrocube had recently got a plug in an FTmarketwatch column by Julie Meyer, co-founder of First Tuesday, the e-world networking outfit. Wilson Harvey, Hoult's agency, used to help organize the First Tuesday parties in London and has assembled the website for Meyer's venture Ariadne Capital. Hoult's sister Anabel had been a classmate of Meyer's at INSEAD Business School, before landing her plum post at Carphone Warehouse.

That business, of course, is headed by Johnson's multimillionaire mates Charlie Dunstone and David Ross, both former pupils at Uppingham school. Hoult went to its great rival, Oundle (Lord Hanson's *alma mater*). All have been known to attend monthly meetings of the Mandrake club, all are affluent, serious professionals who tend to come from well-off backgrounds and feel uncomfortable with too much flaunted wealth. If the new media has a blueblood mafia, they're in it.

Yet on first impressions Hoult seems an unlikely go-getter. Maybe it's the sensible haircut, deferential manner and wide, eager-to-please grin – it seems to hang around his face like a lazy washing line, saying, no worries, nice chap. Wilson Harvey, he tells me, is "the 67th fastest growing company in Britain as rated by Dun & Bradstreet", and then he giggles, as if torn between pride and acknowledging how preposterous such a figure is. It's a charm he uses to great effect, according to others. "Don't be fooled," says Johnson, "underneath it all, Charlie is hugely ambitious."

Sitting in a metrocube meeting room, down in the basement of the building off High Timber Lane in the City, Hoult runs through his background: Newcastle-born, two sisters, eldest son of a father who ran Hoult's, Britain's fourth biggest delivery company, later sold to NFC. Dad went on to run a business park and join Northumberland's great and good. Those who know Charlie Hoult say the family tradition of building businesses and creating wealth runs deep. His father gave him a wodge of NFC shares when he reached 21 to get him started which he sold well for £50,000. He always had schemes going, running clubs at university, putting magazine projects together.

But it took him a decade after school to find his feet. He read English at Manchester University, went to journalism school at Cardiff, did a stint on the London Evening Standard *Londoner's Diary*, which he hated. He dropped out, cycling round Britain to produce a book on the Green lifestyle called *Living Green* – "still available on Amazon" he tells me proudly (and it is).

Then, failing to find a job he wanted, he moved into tech PR and the penny dropped. This was a business with big potential. "Whatever I do, I always have an escape committee going and I thought I could service clients better if I set up on my own." So, with a partner, Paul Burgess, he set up Wilson Harvey with one client and no office. "We called it after our middle names because we wanted it to sound professional but we didn't want to mess up our good names!"

Just as importantly, soon after launching Wilson Harvey he and his sister bought a stack of loss-making tech newsletters (Callcentre Technology, Financial IT, Insurance Technology Report, Financial Marketing). These gave Hoult an entrée into the very profitable world of trade conferences, an area which dovetailed with his experience in nightclub and party organizing.

Charlie Hoult

By 1999 he was nagging the founders of First Tuesday to let him organize some of their networking bashes. John Browning, another First Tuesday co-founder, was impressed. "We were struggling to run these things as they were getting so big and he said, let me try, I do it for a living," says Browning. "And Charlie gets things done, in his own really laid-back way." What tickled him, adds Browning, was that Hoult could be a nightlife king yet actually had rather a tranquil home life, trotting back to his flat in Highbury and his girlfriend, a doctor, as if it was just another day in the office.

Hoult masterminded two of First Tuesday's biggest events, a party at Lord's cricket ground for 1,500 people and a Christmas conference bash at the Fabric nightclub in London's Smithfield, with 2,000 delegates plus a Bob Geldof keynote speech. He later booked Lord's media centre pod for a private party, making 100 invitees wear wigs, beards and paper boiler suits – "everyone was indistinguishable," he remembers. "Boy, did we freak out the bar staff…"

That kind of verve was in big demand during the dotcom boom, though beneath the diffident charm there is evidence of Hoult's determination not to undervalue himself. Ask the founders of First Tuesday why the relationship with Hoult ended and they will tell you they felt his attention was moving elsewhere. As likely an explanation is that Hoult wanted a bigger share of the proceeds for the work he put in. And by then, his ambition was growing.

That was when he started converting the building that housed Wilson Harvey into metrocube. Until recently the site, Sir John Lyon House, used to be a tea-tasting centre where buyers would sample the imported leaves shipped into London. The building's owner, explains Hoult, was going to demolish and redevelop it, taking advantage of its new prominence opposite Tate Modern. Those plans, like the reopening of the Millennium Bridge next door, got delayed and Hoult saw his opportunity.

'I'd sold the newsletters and the money was burning a hole in my pocket," he says. "The agency was growing organically, it doesn't need any cash to keep it going, internet businesses are a hot topic, I thought: let's get one going."

He had worked with a friend on one idea for an e-business, shelved it, looked for something new then realized that the answer was in front of his eyes. He wanted something scalable, synergistic with his agency, which already had one floor in the old Lyon building. Why not refurbish and rent out the rest?

So, not an e-business at all?

"Northern boy likes to sell value, rather than thin air," he sums up for me. Hoult, it should be pointed out, being a posh Geordie, has no trace of an accent, so the northern boy link would be lost on many. But like his father, perhaps, he knows property. Despite the crash in tech stocks and growing doubts about the future of dotcoms, Hoult raised the money for metrocube and negotiated the five-year lease.

There was a real gap in the serviced office market, he reckoned. At one end, the plush Regus offices – "shagpile carpets and paintings on the wall" – that had made founder Mark Dixon a multi-millionaire, at the other the one-off conversions with low technology and bad neighbours. What no-one yet offered was something uncomplicated, with the feel of a club, full of like-minded people, but no advisers pushed upon you, and no unnecessary plush.

So he set about creating it. Floorboards were stripped, decor painted white, partitions installed floor to ceiling with tons of glass, 200 desks on seven floors. It's basic but stylish, the sort of environment a big corporate could never create, with just the necessities catered for: putting milk in the fridge, organizing the cleaners, making sure the air conditioning works, sharing the cost of book-keeping, purchasing, travel arrangements – the kind of things little businesses get snagged by.

"We are the youth hostel to Regus's five-star hotel," says Hoult, widening his smile again. "That doesn't mean a youth hostel isn't full of very intelligent people."

No, Charlie, no.

After the goldrush

By the second time we met, at one of metrocube's incubator evenings (free drinks for tenants in the Samuel Pepys round the corner) Charlie Hoult had just locked out his first tenant for non-payment and looked rather shaken by the experience.

But isn't he being naive? Isn't the real purpose of incubators not to rent space but to get in on promising businesses for next to nothing when they are barely starting? Where's his real profit?

"OK," he says, "we are not saying incubator to everyone. What we can do is pick and choose, we can look at the 20 companies who are in here and choose who is good to work with by watching them. Venture capitalists and other incubators make that call before working with people, and they do it in a vulturish way by saying 'come in, but we want 40%'."

The truth, says another friend, is that for all the talk, Hoult is neither a venture capitalist nor a tech-head, just a sharp businessman with an eye for an opportunity. "With Charlie, part of it is just family, they have a tradition of running good businesses, and part of it is simply curiosity, you know, he thinks: this is shiney and interesting, let's have a go." But if he gets enough metrocubes started, the figures could look very enticing.

Which is probably what attracted a backer like Johnson, 20% owner of metrocube, who freely admits he is more interested in profit than innovation for its own sake. Both men share a background in party-organizing – it was how Johnson, then a medical student, caught the entrepreneurial bug at university – and both move in the same circles.

The problem is, it's hard

"We're both big party-goers so our paths were bound to cross," says Hoult. In fact they met at, of all places, a stag party in Kenya held for a mutual friend. Hoult pitched his idea to Johnson, who was impressed, not least by the idea of the snappy brand combined with a low-cost operation (one of Johnson's business passions).

"Charlie's created a brand that meant something to the kinds of tenants they are after, they see it as added value, it's a great idea," explains Johnson. "So long as he can focus on making it work in a disciplined manner, he will succeed." His comment carries more than a hint of warning. The major investor speaks. Hoult laughs when I tell him and says that Johnson is ultra-competitive, and has never forgiven him for winning at tennis *and* Monopoly when they played. Johnson claims that's not true, the tennis is 1-1 at the moment…

when you're on a roll,

to stop.

The only easy truths are ready clichés

Sometimes you meet someone before they've made it, before they've accumulated the praise, the millions of pounds, and you think – are they really a contender? Sometimes you never know.

Could Hoult roll out the metrocube concept and keep his fingers in all those pies? Could he walk away from at least some of the opportunities now falling his way? The problem is, when you're on a roll, it's hard to stop.

"Like the way he pursued the DTI opportunity, he can now smell these things out," says one of his partners in the regional incubation bid, "and Charlie always wants more. When I said I might have another opportunity, he's been at me ever since like a terrier."

That contacts book, too, was still growing. And round about 2000, says the same source, something definitely clicked. Hoult began to use the same skills he'd honed on his clients to promote himself. "Charlie has this understated persona but I've noticed recently that he's going round, getting his name in various articles, putting himself about. He's got the appetite for it."

It's a dangerous shift – public relations rule number one: never move between your clients and the spotlight – and signalled a step-change in Hoult's ambitions. Less a PR, more an entrepreneur. Others argue that it is hardly surprising. The two are so entwined now. As his sister Anabel says, "Charlie knows" what the media want.

Will Charlie Hoult make millions? Hoult himself laughs it off, implying he's far too nice for that sort of thing. "I come out of a paternalistic small business community, where you hire people, make a bit of money, but you can always go to the annual dinner/dance, and dance with anyone because they don't hate you."

So thus far it's all been a bit of an adventure, nice to get paid along the way, but you've got to keep your interests going outside work, he says, not be totally money-driven. "I want to combine doing all this with the easy life." Plus helping his friends and family, of course. "Can you mention Rob Kelsey's new book, *The Pursuit of Happiness*? He'll love me for ever if you do."

Favours done, obligations created. But where will he be in five years' time? Or ten years? Sometimes the unexpected runs over you like a bus.

Waheed Alli

The first and only time I met Waheed Alli, he was just tasting success as co-producer of *The Big Breakfast* and *The Word*, television shows commissioned by Channel 4. Alli's name never seemed to appear on the credits but, with his boyfriend Charlie Parsons and rock star Bob Geldof, he co-owned the programmes' production company, Planet 24. Those who worked for the shows described him as the managerial and financial brain behind them. He was young, black, gay and, according to others, very ambitious.

A colour supplement asked me to profile him. At first he declined to be interviewed, then, after I dug around Companies House trying to piece together his growing empire of little start-ups, he allowed himself to be persuaded by *Big Breakfast*'s PR firm, Freud Communications. He said he would put aside an hour. In the end he gave me one of the first and (if the amount of calls I've had about it in the past seven years are anything to go by) probably one of the last full-length interviews he's ever done.

Now, of course, he is Lord Alli, Labour peer, exponent of views on issues of race and sexuality and adviser to prime minister and cabinet ministers alike, and someone who, because of the threats he has received – for being black, gay, successful, whatever – doesn't need to promote himself any further in the press. Back then, however, he was a fresh-faced 29-year-old from South Norwood with a background in financial services and magazine publishing, and a natty line in peacock braces, crisp white shirts and wide silk ties.

We met in his office, then a strangely characterless stretch of rented space in a large Docklands block. Outside, flags billowed on poles as if fronting a naff international hotel. In those days, most production companies were based round the watering holes of Soho and Shepherd's Bush, not way out in east London. But that was Alli's nose for a bargain, under-£10 per sq ft; who cares about the bleats from his isolated workforce?

Short, dark and almost too handsome, he sits in an untidy glass box, partitioned off from his finance team. Videos and boxes of merchandizing lie around. Alli looks like a sales manager for a trade mag, all nervous confidence and prepared patter. Then he smiles widely, his black curling hair and fine-featured good-looks testimony to his mixed-race parentage – South American dad, a mechanic, West Indian mother, a geriatric nurse. Back then he had the kind of face that is difficult to read, sleek and taut,

it is not
it's the skills

not yet fattened from years of wealth, only the darting eyes giving away his highly-strung energy.

He already had a reputation as a hard-bastard boss. Those who worked for *Big Breakfast* in its early days talked of 60-hour weeks, pay docked for sick leave, wrangles over contracts. Alli drives people hard and demands respect. There are those in London's tight-knit production world who at that stage think Alli has 'reinvented' himself, claiming a grander background than is actually true. Rumours abound of fortunes made and lost in the City, cash stumped up for the ill-fated Correspondent newspaper, wheeler-dealering in a succession of money-making projects – all at a ludicrously young age, all untrue, and none, I think, spread by Alli himself. But myth and legend cling to the ambitious. The reality is more humdrum but to the press, Alli is a "City whizz" regardless.

In fact it turns out that he has never done anything more glamorous than run a bit of two-day-a-week consultancy in the Square Mile, mainly data

what you do,
you pick up

management, probably not Porsche-driving fare and certainly not an environment in which he enjoyed working. Before that it was a long stint at one of Robert Maxwell's magazine subsidiaries, a few years as a junior at Save & Prosper in the City, and a first job, at 16, as a researcher on *Planned Savings* magazine. He got that from the job centre. But it is not what you do, it's the skills you pick up, he points out coolly. And in television, he found his métier.

It was producer Charlie Parsons who hauled him in, looking for someone to run the business side of his production company while he pitched his *Big Breakfast* idea at Channel 4. They had known each other for years, eventually moving in together, although Alli won't tell me where they met. Parsons' friends at LWT, where he worked on *The Six O'Clock Show*, remembers that in those days Alli called himself Alex, a nickname he later dropped.

"My advice to Charlie at the time," says Alli, "was that he should get a commercial partner because the industry is changing, and if he didn't, he would find himself dragged into running the company at a time when he had to produce things." Parsons' first choice didn't work out, so Alli stepped in and never left. The two are chalk and cheese, of course, but complement each other well. Parsons, a volatile, spikey, Home Counties boy, Tonbridge and Oxford, dad a posh accountant, has a gift for imaginative, tabloid telly. Alli, the smooth-talking organization freak from Stanley Tech in South Norwood, gets off on logistics.

His role as 'facilitator', making possible Parsons' bizarre ideas like shooting *The Big Breakfast* in a three-house knock-through by an East End canal, helped rewrite many of the rules of television. By all accounts, setting up the breakfast show was a nightmare. "If you had told a bunch of hairy-arsed technicians five years ago that you were going to shoot a two-hour daily show in a sitting room with normal ceilings they would have pissed themselves laughing," said Paul Ross, editor of *The Word* and a former *Big Breakfast* presenter. "Then they would have beaten you up…"

Instead Alli doggedly worked it out, craning equipment in, sorting out new ways of working. That's his strength, says Parsons, he learnt his management expertise outside television, and so is not bound by any of the usual television traits. "Television is full of middle-class people who dropped into it for no better reason than that they are not in publishing," says Parsons. "Waheed is able to see things with a clearer view."

He is also the detail man. In those days he spent every Friday beetling across London for the shooting of *The Word*, a controversial (well, pretty awful), late-night youth programme that Planet 24 shot for Channel 4. Alli oversaw the whole production – a fact that is now curiously glossed over – haggling for satellite links, checking the stunts, even though he is never credited. He was, according to one on the show, great at schmoozing the stars and bawling out the agents. He was also frequently the last to leave.

That compensated, say friends, for the fact that he and Parsons had little social life; they were usually too busy. They drove in separately from their house in Islington, Parsons in his Saab 900, Alli in his Ford Granada, always working late. Just once a year Alli's organizational nous and love of glamour combine when he oversees the massive Planet 24 Christmas party. Part PR puff, part staff reward, the production hit its apogee in 1993 when he hired The Ark, then a huge, empty office block in west London, lit the sky with lasers and invited 1,000 media friends. That, of course, was before he became a Labour Lord and had a country seat to invite his mates to.

So there we are, meeting across a small formica table in a nondescript block in Docklands. Alli is simultaneously very courteous and very cautious, putting a small tape recorder beside mine then blushing when he finds out that his tapes, borrowed off his secretary, are only 15 minutes long. It doesn't faze him. Instead, he gets out a long box of tapes and methodically, throughout the conversation, works his way through, continually flipping them out and over, starting again, proving his point, refusing to lose face. By the third or fourth time, the changeover – the coda to our dialogue – is characteristically seamless.

It is 1994, three years before the next Labour government, 15 years since the last one had handed over control and credibility. Fifteen years in which the country had tasted Thatcherism, boom and bust, Majorism, and more – Robert Maxwell drowned and Guinness gone to court, a renewed spirit of entrepreneurialism and the end of jobs-for-life. A different business mindset was beginning to percolate through: less hierarchical, more intuitive, less stuffy, more fly-by-the-seat-of-your-pants. Television production companies led the way. Many of the Branson traits that were feted in the late 90s during the dotcom boom – youth, informality, anything's possible – fuelled the indie production boom of the early 90s, when the government moved to loosen regulatory restraints on commercial television. The winners were those that could carve out some kind of longevity.

Even then, particularly then, Alli seemed to know what he wanted: a breadth of interests in a growing empire. He had plans for merchandizing spin-offs from his shows, moves into magazines and books, he was itching to join lottery consortia and radio franchise bids, he had brought in experienced managers from outside television to oversee the growth. He let Parsons and his team handle the creative side while he focused on getting the bottom line right. And he was nurturing the company's stars, in particular Chris Evans, the ginger-haired presenter whose stint fronting *Big Breakfast* had already captured the media's attention. Evans had set up his own company, Ginger, which Alli clung on to in a characteristically canny way. "I do run it for him, but I work for him, I work as a producer, that's my job," he says with a smile."There's only one difference: I don't have to work for him so it makes it a much more equal relationship."

And more than all that, he had plans, you could see, for how he would use the power of wealth if he ever attained it. He had got a whiff of politics, and he liked it.

I just wish people in industry and

Alli's heroes

I asked Alli if he had any business heroes.

"I don't have any business heroes because they were all icons of the 80s, weren't they? And aren't they all in jail now? The kind of heroes I have are people like Nelson Mandela."

Are politics important in business?

"I think you have to have some ideals and objectives. I'm a card-carrying member of the Labour Party, though I haven't been to a meeting for a couple of years... One of the things I find disturbing is the lack of political objectives in any business. I don't get the sense that these people feel there is something very wrong with our society at the moment because we don't have a decent education system, we don't have a decent health service, we don't have a decent infrastructure, we don't have a proper tax system, we don't have a philosophy about why we are electing governments, that governments are there not to administrate... We've got to have that

there were more

the City

> *that had a conscience*

purpose and objective, we must improve the society we live in. There is no sense of that."

Is that difficult to square with the day-to-day slog of running companies? Hiring, firing, negotiating?

"Not at all. It means you strive to do things, to be the employer you can, you strive to create an environment where ideas can flourish. It means that people don't have to hide their sexuality, that women aren't frightened to take positions of power, that you can walk into an environment where people work together, and against each other at some points, but not in a claustrophobic environment.

"It means that you can be yourself and one of the most satisfying things about this company to me is that it is not a City dealing room. I don't feel frightened about coming here, about who I am, about who I live with and what I do. And people don't have that hierarchical respect you find in other places, oh, that guy is the finance director so I must be nice to him, if they have got something to say, they'll say it.

"Now, if you have got that kind of conscience, you get things wrong and you become a hostage to fortune, and people will throw employment practices at you, but I would much rather have that than not to have a conscience at all like the completely nasty pieces of work that you find elsewhere. I have a conscience. I want to feel guilty about the things I haven't done correctly, and I want to be able to say I have made those mistakes. I have got to feel good about the things that I do. And when I have done them wrong I need to know I have done them wrong. I just wish there were more people in industry and the City that had a conscience."

Aren't there? He gives me an example.

"I went to dinner with some people, and one of them, a City lawyer, said to me, 'oh, it's fashionable to beg now'. And I thought, that is one of the most depressing comments I have ever heard. How can anyone get to the stage where they think it is fashionable to beg on the street? How can he possibly be that wrong about the state of our society? How can he not see that he is exactly the kind of person who will push us into terminal decline? That's why I carry round my Labour Party card. I am not interested in those kind of people any more, and I don't want them around."

Gavyn Davies on Labour in the City

The City of London is an intolerant place, depending on your position. Years later I sit opposite Gavyn Davies, the most unambitious ambitious person you could meet, chief economist at Goldman Sachs, multimillionaire and one-time adviser to Gordon Brown (whose office is run by Davies' wife Sue Nye) and Tony Blair.

He is telling me about his early years in the City. The prodigiously bright only child of working class, academic parents, he had left Oxford to work in a Downing Street policy unit, before leaping into a job as a stockbrokers' economist when Margaret Thatcher became prime minister.

How did a Labour supporter survive in the City during the Thatcherite 80s? Didn't he feel uncomfortable? "No, I was quite open about it," he says. "Anyway, I wasn't ever sympathetic to the bits of the Labour Party that the City was concerned with."

Ah.

Ideals and ambition

But I don't understand, I say to Alli, you've got a reputation in TV-land as a very tough employer, not overgenerous with benefits, rarely easy-going, often aggressive in manner. How easily does that sit next to ideals about aspiring to the kind of work environment you have described?

He is a puzzle.

part-time

Alli barely draws breath. "We do pay sick leave, but we didn't because, like every other independent producer in the country, your employees are on fixed-term contracts. As you know, if you are a schedule D employee, you cannot be paid sick leave, cannot be paid holidays. The Inland Revenue will tell you that. I will only pay people if they are a line employee."

But I wonder if maybe Alli, an outsider to the media who brings in his own experience and management skills, doesn't really like a lot of the people who work there. Alli, in response, rails at the moaners.

"These people are a bit like journalists, they always feel they are being ripped off. They are the kind of people who read their contracts and talk about intellectual property rights. In the real world, in other industries, these are bog-standard contracts and everyone signs them. I use what I thought were standard production contracts, it takes all-rights because I want to own them because it is my programme, I don't want you coming

Part-time entrepreneurial mogul,
political agitator

up and saying that *Big Breakfast* is your idea, and I only do that because I have reciprocal rights with Channel 4. And I only get..." he pauses, "all those intellectual property rights that I have gathered go straight to Channel 4, they don't go into my pocket."

And so the conversation went on: Alli irked at the criticism, and me feeling I was on weak ground because he was right, he wasn't doing anything anyone else wasn't doing, and anyway, none of the whisperers would be quoted on record. Everyone was too frightened of Planet 24's meteoric success. You don't get the next job if you're a moaner.

Years later Alli was ennobled and made millions (probably around £6m) from selling Planet 24 to Carlton for £15m. Carlton's boss, Michael Green, is a committed Conservative supporter. Alli worked at Carlton for a time, helping push through the remake of *Crossroads* (an old childhood favourite of Alli's, apparently), before leaving to join Parsons at a new start-up,

Castaway productions, where they pioneered the Survivor gameshow format and sold it around the world, making them more millions. They clearly have the golden touch.

They have added a big house in the Kent countryside, near the Romney Marsh, to the big house in London. They entertain regularly and lavishly, but generally maintain a low media profile. Alli is broadening his business interests, chairing a consortium that holds one of London's digital radio licences and letting it be known that he would like a non-executive position with a blue-chip FTSE100 firm. He remains a committed Labour supporter, working for the party in the House of Lords.

He is, in short, a puzzle. Part-time entrepreneurial mogul, part-time political agitator. You wonder what he could have achieved if he had set his heart on one, to the exclusion of the other. But then why would he want to do that?

Fashion

Maybe aggressive ambition is out of fashion. All entrepreneurs are ambitious – of course – they just package it differently now. Ambition with moderation, with restraint, with a press embargo, or with a sense of humour. Blame Branson, blame the hippies, blame the New Mexico commune dwellers who became the first techies. No business leader will deny ambition, they will simply dress it up to fit current tastes.

Gerry Robinson's long goodbye

The first time I saw Gerry Robinson he was chief executive of Granada, then a catering-to-television group. We met at his home, a many-million-pound mansion in London's Holland Park. He opened the door himself, casually dressed in shirt, slacks and cardigan, looking tired, big bags under his bright blue eyes – his baby son had been keeping him up late – and, despite the fact it was a weekday and not yet evening, he said he'd been home for a while. He was already hugely rich, the result of a management buy-out at his previous job running Compass catering, and he didn't believe in long working days, he added. His first marriage had collapsed and, as a man starting his second family, he wanted to see as much of his new son and daughter as possible.

It all sounded very reasonable, if unorthodox for a FTSE100 chief executive. He served me tea in his sitting room and he charmed me. I admired his enormous white sofas, the white grand piano, the oil paintings, the view over the garden. He told me there was not much on the horizon for Granada, just consolidation. After all, what could they buy? I left. That was in the summer of 1995. A few months later Granada launched a massive bid for Forte.

All of which led me to suspect that what you get on the surface with Gerry Robinson may not be an accurate reflection of what is going on underneath. When I met him four years later, the sandy hair was a lot greyer, the face a little fuller and the blue eyes a touch faded, but at 50, he was more successful and working harder than ever. By then he was chairman of Granada, earning £1m a year to add to his £15m Compass cashpot, and he had not lost his capacity for surprise, either. After proving a late convert to Tony Blair's New Labour, he had caused consternation in the arts world by accepting the government's invitation to become chairman of the Arts Council.

This, remember, was the accountant-turned-manager who, famously, was faxed "fuck off out of it, you upstart caterer" by John Cleese when he ousted David Plowright from the top of Granada TV in 1991. Only months after joining the Arts Council, Robinson was, of course, in the process of dismantling and re-organizing it.

He has also pledged his future to Granada after continual speculation that he might be leaving. Yet at the same time he had sold the many-million-pound mansion, bought a flat round the corner, and quietly moved his

Gerry Robinson

young family from London to Donegal, where he was born – not the actions of an ambitious man chasing more challenges over here. He commuted from Ireland's north-west coast, where he owned both a cottage and a big house and where his children go to school. That, you feel, must take some commitment.

"Oh, the travelling is a pain," he agreed, looking, unusually for Robinson, rather glum.

There were clearly compensations, though. He was sitting at his desk beside the vast windows in his first-floor office at Granada's base in St James. The office is sumptious, tall and wide, with a long view over Green Park and Buckingham Palace. The room is arranged with pleasing precision. His desk and chair sit in the window flanked by two giant jungle plants. Opposite him, four chairs are lined up like penitent beggars. By the fireplace, two rows of plain leather sofas huddle over a low coffee table. Every fitting, every standard light, every chair appears to be a work of art. A gorgeous Ben Nicholson abstract, part of the Granada collection, hangs on the wall in front of him. Anyone who thinks Robinson is an austere, cost-chiselling accountant should come and look at this.

I ask him what this half-here, half-there approach means. Ireland, England, pretending to be laid back while adding more commitments. Was he masking his ambition, or was he actually playing out a sort of Long Goodbye? He's going, he's gone, but he's actually still here doing more than ever before?

"Ha!" he laughs. "Yup, bit like Frank Sinatra."

Robinson laughs easily, great, breathy gusts of giggles that often catch you by surprise. It is his easy-going sense of humour that those who meet him note first. His elder brother John, who headed the construction firm Trollope and Colls, says that the Robinsons have always been a family of Mickey-takers. "We are either getting upset or taking the piss," he says, laughing too, when I ring him up.

They are a famously large family. Robinson is one of ten born to a Donegal carpenter and his tough, Glaswegian wife (nee Stewart). They left Ireland when Robinson was nine and moved to London's East End. There was little money, dad worked on building sites, but mum ran the family with real management precision, and was ambitious for her children, especially bright little Gerry, born ninth, who was sent to a seminary but eventually chose accountancy over the priesthood. They have all done well, "but Gerry was always keen to learn a bit more than the next person," remembers John. He had a quick wit, a brilliant head for figures and, more pertinently, mum's genius for delegation.

Now forget the humour. Those outside the business world have a very different view of Robinson. This curious form of double vision was well illustrated by a 1998 television documentary about the Granada/Forte takeover battle. Bizarrely, it depicted Robinson as a cold, humourless roundhead endlessly preoccupied with reducing payrolls, and Sir Rocco Forte as a warm, lovable cavalier who put his staff before everything.

it depicted Robinson

preoccupied with

(Some who worked for Forte remember it rather differently but that's another story.) *The Guardian* had another shot at it a year later, heading a potted biography of Robinson: RUTHLESS CHARMER FROM HUMBLE IRISH STOCK. Note the large dollop of British class consciousness.

"Hmm, makes me sound like a recipe, doesn't it?" says Robinson smoothly, regaining his humour. He has, it seems, a quip for everything.

In truth, many people cannot make him out at all. To some, he *is* the recipe for millennium success: modest, committed, self-deprecating, and very much not of the old Establishment. And despite his run-of-the-mill executive experience – he started as a cost clerk at Lesney Toys, and worked his way through finance positions at Lex and Grand Met's Coca-Cola franchisee subsidiary before moving into senior management – he has always had that quality which many British-born company men lack: charisma. He acts like an entrepreneur, even though his success has been purely old-fashioned-corporate. You feel it the moment you engage with

as a cold, humourless roundhead

reducing payrolls

him, the attention to detail, the soft charm, the infectious good humour. It is said he was something of a ladies' man in his early years, and you can quite believe it, especially as he doesn't exactly discourage the impression. There are the endless jokes about why he left the seminary, and the admission that his first marriage broke up because he was unfaithful.

So, was he a terrible womaniser?

"Yeah, in the sense I was never very good at it!" he shouts, eyes twinkling, nearly falling backwards off his chair with laughter. It's all loud enough for you to know it's not a straight denial. Then, seriously, he adds that the first time he got married he was too young, just 21. "And if you have been locked away in a seminary, you have got a bit of time to make up."

The bantering charm cuts both ways, however. Business rivals are infuriated by his popularity in the City, and especially the insouciant image he promotes. Why does he have to do that? they rage. One media mogul attended a press lunch on the day that Granada's bid for Forte was announced and could barely contain his glee, declaring to journalists that this time Robinson was definitely in the mire. Definitely. *Schadenfreude* wasn't the half of it…

But the bid went through, of course, and Robinson's Teflon coating remained unchipped. Others find his easy-going accessibility impossible to square with the rigorous efficiency of his managerial regimes. They cite low morale among Granada staff, in particular how the niggardliness of the financial demands squeezes any humanity out of its television arm. At one time, worker discontent there was continually threatening to spill over into strike action.

No-one in the City cares about worker happiness, though. They say, just look at the figures. In less than eight years Robinson had turned a loss of £110m at Granada in to profits of £700m-plus. On that basis, every company could do with a Robinson. Few executives developed so large and faithful a following in the City. That magnetism seemed to work its power on Britain's Labour politicians too.

Whether his time at the Arts Council has been a success, I will leave you to judge. I will offer only this. When I ask Robinson: won't he acknowledge that the work-shy image is something of a pose now? He simply shakes his head.

"If something comes up that requires seven-day working, then I will do it. But it rarely does. I think a lot of people just use work as a way of not confronting themselves."

Graffito on an entrepreneur's wall

Ambition: I want to be what I was when I wanted to be what I am now...

SMART LUCK

But most of all I want to be lucky

WHILE WRITING ABOUT AN AMERICAN IN THE SPRING OF 2000,
I get talking on the phone to a West Coast editor. I don't really understand,
I say, I know everything is booming out there, Silicon Valley going crazy,
money thrown around like tinsel etc etc but why is this guy so successful?
It doesn't stack up. Is he just lucky?

She laughs and says, "We have a phrase for it out here that we use a lot
right now: smart luck. That's him."

I like the phrase so much I want to make it my own.

Dan Wagner isn't

Dan is a man who needs two hands to count all the schools he went to but
he's used to ploughing on, confidently, blindly, convincingly. For years it
worked but right now, he's re-experiencing an unusual feeling: failure. "It's
been a catalogue of fucking disasters, hasn't it?" he says, the cocksure
sheen draining from his face. He is describing how debt and bad publicity
tore the heart from his global infotech company. So he's sold off the bulk of
it and he's starting again. He never gives up. "I still see myself as being very
creative... I have a good understanding of the tech market, I'm very
plugged into the tech community, I can identify opportunities that others
haven't seen, I have demonstrated that again and again..."

Some make it, others don't. Smart luck, that is.

Charlie Dunstone has an e-mail

"Hi Charles, I liked your picture and profile in one of the recent magazines
and took a fancy to you..."

He's reading it out to me from the screen on his desk, a look of bemused
wonder on his chubby face. At 36, unmarried, worth an estimated £600m
or so, Dunstone is one of the most eligible entrepreneurs in Britain.

"…I wondered if you were dating anyone. If not, can I take you out?"

Dunstone, founder and chairman of Carphone Warehouse (CPW), who *is* dating someone, looks at me and shrugs as if to say, what can you do? The world is weird.

Well, be careful when you invite customers to e-mail the boss, I guess.

"Yeah," says Dunstone, reading on, "according to my IT rep, he is forwarding my home phone number, address and vital statistics…"

He chuckles, shaking his head but clearly flattered. Dunstone and his old schoolchum David Ross, chief operating officer of CPW, are getting used to this now. Having created one of the most successful British retail businesses of the past decade, floated on the Stock Exchange in 2000 with a market cap of £1.7bn, they get a lot of offers coming their way. Politicians, media, charities, gold-diggers. And all from just being good at selling mobile phones. It must be strange, waking one morning and finding yourselves the Glam Duo of entrepreneurial Britain.

If you leave school with

you've got

Ross, 35, the more taciturn of the two, the money man, just shrugs at that sort of question, as if to say, introspection? That's Charlie's field.

And he's right. Dunstone, the marketing whizz, the man who trades on charm and honesty – Ross says Charlie is good at selling "because he's so personable" – is up for it.

"What's funny," he says, returning to the sofa in his first-floor, west London office, "is that I'm not really an incredibly self-confident person, I am quite introspective and self-critical, you know, I am just sitting here in Acton working away. Then sometimes I go and make a speech and listen to them introducing me, and think, is that right? I suppose so, but it's quite odd…"

Even odder is Dunstone and Ross's background: both public schoolboys from business-rich backgrounds, Dunstone's dad a big wheel at BP, his grandad a City blueblood and former Cazenove consultant, and Ross's family responsible for the famous frozen food company of the same name.

ew qualifications

nothing to lose

That's how entrepreneurial Britain has changed. These kind of well-off guys just don't build massive companies from scratch – 1,000 Carphone Warehouse stores in Britain, over 600 on the Continent – they become lawyers, accountants, drop-outs, don't they?

"I've a theory about that," says Dunstone, little dark eyes twinkling. "If you leave school with few qualifications, you've got nothing to lose and you're quite happy to go and set up a business…" Hence his own background, never shining academically, deciding it wasn't worth taking up his place at Liverpool University, getting jobs in computer sales and then flogging phones to NEC's corporate customers.

"…If you're more successful then you go and join Arthur Andersen or something" – which is what his mate Ross did before Dunstone lured him out, just as he qualified, to join his little start-up.

"I tell you," says Dunstone, "everyone at Andersen's thought David was nuts to join me here when we started. Me, I was working as a salesman before, and if this hadn't worked out, I could have got a very similar job and would have lost absolutely nothing." Rosso, as he calls him, was much the braver, even if his gamble has now paid off hugely. But that's what you have to do if you want to make it as entrepreneurs, whatever your background: gamble and leap.

Dunstone and Ross have a tight relationship, one of the closest in British business, forged from their days at Uppingham school. Dunstone insists I interview both of them, making sure the emphasis is on the team, not just on one man. It's pretty smart, consistent with the company's emphasis on spreading responsibility around, stressing motivation and incentive, and with Dunstone's assurance that he has no desire to be the new Richard Branson. Personal publicity helps, he says, especially in a world awash with mobile phone shops (The Link, Vodafone Retail, DX Communications, Pocket Phone) but…

"It doesn't take too long before someone who has developed high public awareness gets a good kicking and that has a negative impact on the organization, so you've got to have balance."

Ross, of course, brushes aside any hint of premeditation. Charles wants me to have more credit? I wouldn't know about that, he says. "I think you are reading a lot more into it than is really involved."

And that's his style. Chunkier, better looking, with a handshake that could crack walnuts, Ross gets enough publicity anyway, having set up home with Will Carling's dumped girlfriend Ali Cockayne. The redtops love it, millionaire business tyro sweeps sad Ali off her feet, leading you to think that the Carphone duo's press strategy is always within a whisker of being knocked off kilter. Even Dunstone was forced to giggle last year: "I do the broadsheets, David does the tabloids", a quote that seemed to have escaped his business partner.

"Did Charlie really say that?" says Ross gruffly when I put it to him. He has the kind of sandpaper-worn voice that sounds as if it would be happiest screaming at a scrum of rugby players. "Cheeky bugger…"

Both men like to banter and are clearly hewn from the same wood: short, broad, mousey blonds, eldest sons in their respective families, but with rather different strengths. Cambridge-born Dunstone, with only a kid sister for competition, was always chatty and easy-going, despite a strict upbringing. His parents spent a lot of time abroad – his father ran BP's Danish subsidiary for a while before heading the company's consumer products division. Young Charles was used to looking after himself. Most of all, he loved selling stuff at school, buying in lighters and tat from the back of Exchange & Mart and illicitly selling them on with 100% mark-up (one of his salesmen was schoolmate, now TV star, Johnny Vaughan). Dunstone's teen nickname was Stubber – he says it was because his name sounded like Dunhill, others say it was because he smoked so much.

Charlie Dunstone

Grimsby-born Ross, much the sportier, more competitive, comes from a bigger family and has tougher edges. His parents divorced, his father married three times, there were lots of kids. "One brother, three sisters, one step-sister, one step-mother, that sort of stuff," says Ross.

"I don't really want to get into my family background," he adds, with a cold edge, "but one thing I will say, coming out of a split family means you have to rely on your own wits and make your own decisions a lot earlier than you would if your parents were happily married." His father and grandfather had run their own businesses – Ross frozen foods was sold to Imperial Tobacco, then broken up by Hanson – he always wanted to do the same, leaving Andersen's was never difficult. It is his restless drive which, according to others at the company, has pushed Dunstone to expand ever onwards.

Yet no-one is really sure what alchemy these two tapped into creating their multimillion-pound fortunes. Talk to Dunstone's father, now retired, and he will tell you that his son's success is no surprise to him: Charles may not have excelled academically but even as a child, he had a phenomenal memory and good technical ability – fixing fridges, fiddling with pipes, putting electronics together – plus that gregarious plausibility. "At the age of seven," says Denis Dunstone, "Charles could hold a dining table of adults spellbound with his telling of funny stories."

Others say the key is in how Dunstone and Ross work together. Dunstone started CPW in 1989, but it was only after Ross joined in 1991 that it really took off. Dunstone did front office, running the team; Ross, better at figures, did the back, identifying new sites, telling his partner how much he could spend, sorting out cash flow, ensuring there was money. That is where most start-ups fail: cash flow blips, staff don't get paid, kaput.

Then what began as "just a crazy scheme to have a few shops, 12 at most" (Ross) became a serious money-chase, as the company raced to keep ahead of the giants in a rampant retail market. How did established chains like Dixons let them get away with it? They just didn't see the wave coming, and Dunstone and Ross surfed the initial demand for mobiles from the self-employed better than anyone else. Why phones? Ross laughs and says it was "a natural progression for Charlie, from school lighters to mobiles, the next hot product".

What's doubly curious is how those public school roots still permeate through the business, now a multinational operating in 15 countries Europe-wide. There are no less than six Uppingham alumni in the management team, and the ethos, according to one who deals with them, is rather male and "rugger-buggery". Yet it's imperceptible to customers, as Dunstone and Ross have managed to bind together a multi-ethnic workforce of men and women from very different social backgrounds.

Dunstone, acknowledging that it is deeply unfashionable to say it, attributes much of his business nous to what he learnt at boarding school. "It teaches you to get on with people, you learn about human behaviour, but especially it breeds a Colditz spirit which is fantastically strong. When

London analyists fear

might go down

someone puts an obstruction in front of you, you think, no, I am not going to take it, I am going to find a way around."

In business, he says, you can create the same spirit of "us against the establishment".

"I am such a firm believer that people really over-rate the differences that gender and ethnic background mean. If you've got a strong culture and drive to achieve things, that's motivation to any human being, and that's what we try to achieve."

So who is the establishment? "Oh, not one person or thing," he says, "but you know, the landlord who won't rent you the shop or the manufacturer who won't sort out the service procedure, or whatever."

And all that's reinforced with regular staff bonding, monthly pub evenings, an annual fancy dress staff ball with suppliers and friends invited, then

hat one day, these guys

in a flaming wreck

everyone – and there are over 5,000 staff now – encouraged to get ripped once the outsiders go home. "It's all based around team spirit and a sense of equality," says Ross, "rather than doffing caps and addressing Charles as Mr Dunstone."

Happy staff make happy customers, especially as CPW positions itself as the chain to go to if you want independent, impartial advice (many of its rivals are owned by mobile networks). And Dunstone is very good at sensing what staff and customers want, hence the chain's no-nonsense leaflets on health hazards, managing costs, explaining WAP (wireless application protocol) and so on.

Now the team are trying to squeeze all this into a vehicle as conservative as a plc. The shift to float the company, something which Dunstone spent much of the late 90s agonizing over, came with the expansion into Europe, masterminded by Ross. "When we had success on mainland Europe and wanted to roll it out faster, we had to float," says Dunstone. "If you step off the plane in Milan as a private company, there is a feeling of 'who the hell are you? Some little English mobile phone dealer?' You have to raise your profile."

Selling off chunks of their ownership made the duo even richer (their combined personal fortunes, including the 60% stake they kept in CPW, exceeded £1bn in January 2001) and enabled them to give more of the company out to the staff – though not, some whisper, over-generously. They are using the capital raised to open more shops, set up their own services, all this at a pace that engenders a certain nervousness among London analysts, some of whom fear that one day, these guys might go down in a flaming wreck, especially as they are linked to a telecoms sector which went into freefall in early 2001.

Even Dunstone admits that, as a retailer, they are hostage to what products and services happen next, and whether innovations like the wireless internet take off. "We are at the bottom of the food chain," he says. "If everyone above us screws up, there's little we can do about it." But when we met, after booming sales over Christmas 2000, the telecoms turbulence had yet to even dent their revenue.

And building quickly is what has defined their success. "We were always ahead of the game in that we thought the mobile phone industry was going to fly," says Ross. And crucially, when they need it, they always seem to get lucky. Ross cites a couple of brilliant shop deals early on in CPW's history, rent-free in Oxford Street and Lakeside during the 1993/4 property slump, as a key pump-primer. Others cite their ability to mess up, as with their attempt to sell digital cameras through the 36-shop Techno chain – a joint venture with Mandrake chums Luke Johnson and Julian Richer – and yet get out covering their costs.

Just as crucially, they have found a way of working together that engenders trust, and discourages factionalism. Des Wilson, CPW non-exec, who describes Dunstone and Ross as "probably the two most brilliant, hard-working and committed young people I have ever worked with", says their loyalty to each other is extraordinary. "Cross one, and you cross them both."

The new me

A few miles across town, staring at the carpet in a little meeting room off the foyer of his West End office, Dan Wagner wipes a hand down his face. He pulls himself together. Self-absorption is not Wagner's natural mode. Happy in his own company, slightly insecure among others, over-compensating with too much confidence, too much assurance – that's his style.

For every up, there's a down. For every Dunstone, there's a Wagner. Similar start, same affluent background, but Wagner's story, the man who made it, lost it and is trying again, provides a telling commentary on the flipside of bright, new, entrepreneurial Britain.

Dan Wagner

Set up his first infotech company at 21, floated it at 31, made the mega-takeover deal when he was 34, crippled by debt before he was 36. In 2000, aged 37, he surprised everyone by selling off the bulk of his company Dialog's business and setting up afresh as the tiny (well, £8.5m turnover) Bright Station plc. When we meet in early 2001, Wagner, a naturally ebullient, some would say irritatingly assured performer, seems chastened by the whole experience.

"The eight or nine years after I started my first company were awful…"

Why?

"Because of the stigma of being a ceo younger than 30. Ridiculous if you think about it. I was 15 years too soon. Then I got criticized for being 30 when we floated, but I'd been running the company for 10 years…"

And do you feel others don't appreciate your qualities?

"There is a terrible stigma about me in the financial media, because I was a real pain in the arse to them. I took them to court, I took them to the MMC…"

Wagner believes his rivals in the online information business, many of them global media giants, allowed competition to get the better of objectivity when it came to reporting his actions.

"I tell you, if you're going to be a public company, the last thing you want to do is compete with the two media giants that control perception of your stock, Reuters and the *Financial Times*. You know?"

And that has affected people's perception of you?

"If people in the City who I have never met think I am a flash git, then I suppose so."

Do you find that depressing?

Driving away in
he left an

"No, it's not depressing, I don't care if people like me or not, I just care about the people I know…"

Wagner slumps back in his chair, torn halfway between petulance and self-pity. At times like this, it is hard not to feel sorry for him, hard to see what he did wrong. The son of a successful car industry executive, he left school at 16 with barely a handful of O levels, parlayed early jobs with Julian Richer and WCRS advertising into a vision for his own start-up, MAID, a supplier of online research for businesses. He set it up, fought off stiff competition, developed it into a public company, one of the first to take its business information service onto the internet, he amassed a share fortune worth £40m, and then…

Then, as he sees it, he was "fucking hammered" – nicely put, Dan – for the personal qualities that have underpinned his business drive. Young¿ Brash¿ Mouthy¿ Jewish¿ Qualities which, in America, would barely have got him

his Aston Martin

indelible impression:

flash git

noticed above the scrum of noisy money-makers. But over here, oh no, we do things differently.

The other reading, of course, is that if you promise results, and don't deliver, you do eventually get hammered, however far you've come, whatever religion you practise. And if you bad-mouth your rivals, as Wagner did continuously on his way up, they get even when you're vulnerable. Welcome to the world of grown-up business. Now, after selling his core business, Wagner says he is going to give it one last try in the public arena. He has kept the technology assets of his old firm, relaunched the whole lot as Bright Station, split that into five, brought in professional managers to run the different bits, has plans to float off the successful divisions without his involvement.

And that's all part of the new style. He's changed, he says, he's married, had a kid, he's settling down. He's going to stop criticizing the City, stop blaming his advisers, stop chasing headlines, let go of the thing with the FT and Reuters, watch what he says, resist the urge to slag off Autonomy, his new rival, just get on with keeping his head down and managing the new business.

"This is the new me," he laughs, "the new uncontroversial me, I've taken the pills, I'm much more mellow."

Really?

"Yeah," he shrugs, "it comes from seven years as a public company ceo and the appalling share price performance in that period. It makes you realize: just go grey!"

And for a minute he is very convincing.

The odd thing is how little he has changed since I last met him back in the bumptious 80s. Now, sitting in a first-floor meeting room at Bright Station's Leicester Square headquarters, he has the same oiled-back hair, the smirky grin, the darting eyes, the drapey suit over the lean frame. Not a trace of grey. Only the face looks older, slightly jowlier, more melancholy when he's not smiling – reflecting, perhaps, that half-a-lifetime of business experience packed into his early years.

Back in the 80s, you didn't meet many 21-year-old entrepreneurs. Wagner had the arena to himself, and probably suffered from that. But even then, there was something desperate about him, about his determination to get to the top, to make money, to be recognized. In my life, that impacted as a desperation to get written about: he'd send something, he'd ring, he'd drive round to my office. He was charming but incorrigible, like one of those kids who is told that everything they do is wonderful, and becomes completely insensitive to how others feel or perceive them. But as a young man who was simultaneously pushing his business in London and New York, that is how he had learned to be, the very opposite of retiring. Unfortunately, it never really worked with a British audience. Driving away in his Aston Martin he left an indelible impression: flash git.

Still got the Aston Martin?

"Yeah I've still got it," says Wagner, face creasing into another wide smile. There are times, you guess, when it takes him a little longer than most to catch on to the subtler nuances. Then he twigs: "I am enthusiast, I didn't buy it 'cos I'm a flash git!" And to prove it, guess what he called his daughter? Aston Wagner...

Ah.

So can Dan Wagner change? Should Dan Wagner change?

Many who know him well are not that convinced that he can. Wagner, they say, is a package, you get the lot, good and bad: ambition, drive, a fantastic nous for technology, for being able to see what might come next, but combined with a fervent desire to talk everything up, to get noticed, to prove his worth, to shout the story from the highest rooftop. Asking him to keep quiet is not a reasonable request.

"He's a visionary, make no mistake, and he's a nice guy, but I don't believe the new Dan bit," says one who has worked closely with him. "There have been several rebirths, lasting about six months. The problem is, you are dealing with personal characteristics and they tend not to alter."

And where did he get those characteristics? No-one's quite sure. Perhaps from his father, John Wagner, former executive at Lex's Volvo UK dealership, and md of first VW Audi's, then BMW's British subsidiaries. Physically very similar, father and son share the same determination and ebullience, according to those who know both, although Wagner senior tends to temper his with more gravitas in public. He ended up running his son's American operation and got to see first-hand the difficulties Dan would talk himself into. According to one former colleague, he would be as exasperated as any but could do little about it. Dan points out that his dad "made millions" out of an initial investment in MAID, so he probably doesn't have too much to complain about. "Everyone made millions... I'm the only one who never really cashed in," he shrugs.

if you don't push loudly, steamroller

Wagner cites his father as one of the key influences on his life. Born in Edgware in 1963, the youngest of two brothers (his elder sibling now runs an investment fund in New York), Wagner remembers being "enamoured by the trappings" of his father's business life from an early age: presentations by ad agencies at the family home, articles in the business press. "I was always really interested in it, particularly the advertising thing, my father had a very strong marketing background."

In most respects it was a conventional, north London, Jewish upbringing, more liberal than orthodox. Then when Wagner was nine, his parents divorced, he stayed with his mother, but his father's business success remained the chief pull. After failing to find a groove at a succession of schools, culminating in a miserable period at a crammer – "things I didn't enjoy I just didn't do, as simple as that" – Wagner left to become a photographer's assistant at 16.

others will just *over you*

That, he decided, was too much of a long slog, so he took a job at Julian Richer's first hi-fi shop in London Bridge. Richer, who has now made a name for himself as a retail guru with a gift for staff motivation and, of course, has worked with Dunstone, remembers the teenage Wagner as "very bright, very entrepreneurial". Wagner says his stint with Richer gave him the confidence to think he could make it. One of Wagner's initiatives made Richer thousands of pounds: claiming back the cost of minor repairs off manufacturers' warranties. Richer offered Wagner a shop managership but his young assistant had other ambitions: getting into advertising. He designed and delivered a poster advertising his talents to Robin Wight, founder of WCRS, who took him on as a runner for £2,500 a year. It was less than he was getting from Richer but it gave him his foot in the door.

He put on a suit every day, he got noticed, he got promoted. A job in research led to a role in a BT campaign advertising the future potential for data communication online – this when the IBM pc was just taking off – and PLICK! Wagner's lightbulb went on. If you could put all the market reports and research online, new business departments in ad agencies would pay a premium for access. He was still only 20. Yet he left to set it all up.

Why? Why him of all the people who must have been associated with that campaign, working for the agency or the client? Virtually anyone working in the information or technology businesses would have had more experience, more access to funding, more contacts than him. He was a barely-out-of-teens loudmouth with virtually no GCSEs and two years' experience in a hi-fi shop. Why him?

It was, it seems, the usual mix of chance, naivety and chutzpah. WCRS hadn't given him the pay rise he wanted and he was angry. He had a point to prove, wanted to be his own boss and had no idea of the scale of competition that faced him. And when he did start working on his idea, he got even angrier with the people who tried to take it away. Wagner tells one story which pretty much sums up what he faced: a data company that listened to his pitch, invited him in to work on the project, then nicked his idea.

"This guy completely took the piss out of me. I did all this work with him, then he came to see me for a drink in the Churchill Hotel and I will never forget it. He said: 'Thanks, Dan, I just want you to know that we've had this idea for a long time, you know, and we are prepared to give you £20,000 to walk away'. And I was completely confused, I said, 'I don't understand'. Then I realized, and thinking on my feet, I said, 'make it £100,000 and you've got a deal'. And he stood up and said, 'I'll meet you in the marketplace' and he walked off. I sat there completely stunned."

For the boy who had been given a torrid time at school, who was never going to fit in to someone else's corporate hierarchy, yet who desperately wanted the same respect and success his father had enjoyed, such treatment could only have confirmed his gut feelings: if you don't push loudly, others will just steamroller over you.

So by sheer belligerence and force of personality, Wagner got on with setting up on his own, raising money, selling to clients not just in the UK but in America, France and elsewhere. And because bigger rivals were racing for the lead, he was in a hurry. If his pushiness wound up some he encountered, he didn't have time to notice.

Until it all started to go wrong. Perhaps his real mistake was taking the company public, giving him shareholders and the City to answer to. Wagner thinks they disliked his youth. Others say he simply lacked judgement. He was sharp, but never smart, either about his rivals, or the media. A London analyst told the Wall Street Journal in 2001 that Wagner's problems were always about leadership: "We keep coming back to the same issue, the bloke running the show. He's long on ideas and announcements and short on the figures."

Wagner wails: "But this guy has never met me!" Yet it was certainly his reputation that tipped the boat when, after his audacious purchase of the American giant Knight Ridder Information for £280m in 1997, taking on a load of debt in the process, his luck ran out. The new outfit, which he renamed Dialog (after KRI's biggest product), failed to hit the promised revenue targets, Wagner lost credibility with his lending banks – he was badly advised on the loans, he says – and his whole team watched aghast as their reputation and share price were shredded. Floated at 110p, up to £3, then woosh – by early 2001 Bright Station plc, formerly Dialog plc, formerly MAID plc, was trading below 40p.

What frustrates Wagner was that they missed their targets by so little. "Knight Ridder was in terminal decline. We had said we would increase revenues by 10%. I admit it was a hell of a story for people to buy. That was a mistake, setting targets we wanted to achieve without providing a suitable buffer, we could have been a lot more lenient on ourselves, but we achieved a reduction in our cost base, we halted the decline in revenue, we improved it one or two per cent, and then we got hell. Profit came in at $63m and we should have got $68m. When take the interest out, we should have made $15m and made $7m, OK, but we were fucking hammered.

"It wouldn't have been so bad on its own but we had spent all our time in the US with our sleeves rolled up, we didn't have someone in London communicating our progress to the press and analysts, maintaining knowledge of where we were, the markets weren't prepared for any variance. Within five minutes of the results going out Reuters put out a note with a headline saying Dialog in danger of breaching banking covenants, absolute nonsense, nowhere near covenant levels, and people said shit, they're going to go bust!"

But it was more than just bad luck. Michael Mander, who worked for Thomson and Hill Samuel before joining Wagner as MAID chairman in 1987, says there was simply too little goodwill to draw on. "The problem was that Dan had a compulsive urge from the start to twist the tails of the lions around him. And it never stopped."

That "twisting" took the form of over-optimistic market share and revenue promises, continual needling of competitors, and a yen for press coverage that exasperated everyone.

But isn't that what entrepreneurs are supposed to do? Fight the fight, create the myth?

Another former colleague, Ciaran Morton, who went on to become Dialog's president of Europe, Middle East, Africa and Asia Pacific, explains that initially it was all done with a purpose: to generate more column inches than their larger database rivals. But eventually Wagner simply enjoyed it too much, and didn't realize quite what damage he was doing to his reputation. "Dan just loved to get a headline."

And sometimes the headlines were good. Dialog was heavily plugged by *The Mirror*'s City team – sell your grandmother, buy these shares – and Wagner was regularly feted by the tabloids as a hot techie to watch. So can he complain just because the headlines turned against him? He says so, and claims competitors like Reuters and the FT had a vested interest in running him down. He points out that the biggest nail in the coffin of his ambitions came when the FT's respected Lex column snidely dubbed the company 'Dialadog'.

"They ran it one day," says Wagner, "then the next day they had it again, in case you didn't get it the first time!" He got hammered for wearing a Donald Duck waistcoat to a presentation, City editors leapt on the bandwagon criticizing his judgement. In fact, Wagner had been getting it in the neck since the company floated. Something about him clearly wound up the City establishment – Wagner can still quote the pertinent pieces.

"One commentary before the pricing, headed THIS MAID IS NEITHER FAIR NOR WHOLESOME ended with the words, 'God help pension fund managers for investing in this one'. Their main objection just seemed to be that I was confident and young!"

Really? Surely the constant chatter in the press was part of it. One MAID executive remembers a broker saying to him: "If you could only shut Wagner up, the share price would double overnight".

OK, says Wagner, his American-style drive – always take the calls, always up for the battle – may have made Brits uneasy. "But you don't make it in New York without being incredibly aggressive in your sales approach, especially if you didn't have any money. In the UK I used to carry two business cards, Dan Wagner salesman and Dan Wagner ceo, because people here didn't think I could be both. In America they thought I was great!"

And it's true, search the cuttings and you will find very little adverse comment in America on Wagner's personal style. Morton, who worked with Wagner for ten years, says he is not blind to his old boss's faults – "he is a competent man-manager but always more interested in putting things together" – yet he's hardly the spiv he's portrayed as. Worse, Morton suggests there may have been an element of anti-semitism behind the whole 'Dialadog' campaign. To some in the City, Wagner's brash, Gordon Gekko approach made him fair game. "How often do you see defamatory versions of company names in papers like the FT? Hardly ever, I think," says Morton. (Actually, market nicknames are used increasingly in comment pieces.)

But maybe some of it was just timing. Back in the early 90s, the market wasn't ready for impossibly young ceos of public companies dealing in cutting edge technology. "If he'd launched MAID at the beginning of 2000 no-one would have blinked," Andrew Chapman at Bright Station's broker ABN Amro, told me. "Being first out of the box attracted the attention… and I think Dan learnt from that."

Meaning: he *hopes* Dan learnt from that.

while the company is growing

quibble about their

Chaps

Perhaps the moral is that true entrepreneurs shouldn't tangle with plc investors. If you need smart luck to succeed in business, maybe public offerings, the demands of shareholders, the scrutiny of analysts and the press, just diminish its potency. They grind you down. They mould you into conformity.

Younger bosses have learnt from Branson, from Roddick: you bridle against the constraints of London's Square Mile, you lose. You break rules, you lose. You fail to make the right noises, or look the right type, you lose. Is it just because they're not the right kind of chaps¿

Luck: the action or effect of casual or uncontrollable events; the sum of fortuitous events affecting (favourably or unfavourably) a person's interests or circumstances; a person's apparent tendency to have good or ill fortune; the imagined tendency of chance to bring a succession of (favourable or unfavourable) events...

(OXFORD ENGLISH DICTIONARY)

fast, no-one is going to

lifestyles

Reasoned charm

Back in north Acton, Charlie Dunstone makes all the right noises. The move to being a listed company is not a problem, he says, it just ensures you put in proper systems and it stops you getting complacent. "You've got to continue to deliver and exceed people's expectations, it requires you to be continually inventive."

And Branson and Roddick?

"I think we are more pragmatic and business-like than Branson and Roddick. Not less idealistic, just more realistic." Hence, perhaps, the sudden disappearance of one Ernest Saunders, former Guinness chief, from the list of CPW advisers. Saunders, disgraced in the Guinness scandal, whose children are friends of Dunstone's, helped the duo a lot in the company's early years but once the City was involved, he was out. People learn, people move on.

Even so, there are indications that the new scrutiny may yet needle Dunstone and his partner Ross. When I ask why there are so few women among CPW's senior management, and none on the board, Ross looks at me suspiciously.

"Not enough women, who says that? We did have a lady operations director on the board…" but she left. Dunstone admits they have been "pretty bad" at external recruitment, much better at promoting from within. "And the people who tend to stick it out have been male, rather than female."

Then there is the examination of the personal, the running tabs on how much Dunstone is spending on his yachts (his favourite hobby) or Ross on his new houses (a large one in London's Cadogan Square plus a stately home with 100 acres in Leicestershire), the strange e-mails and begging letters that are trickling in – it all adds to the pressure. "This one," says Dunstone, fishing more paper off his desk, "is asking me to buy them a house because they don't want to pay the interest on a mortgage. It's got a bloody indoor swimming pool!".

But they're business icons now and times have changed. Two years before, when I had last met Dunstone, sitting rather morosely on his office sofa, staring out at his rain-soaked car park, he had made great play of the fact that there were "no Porsches", no fancy cars, no business lunches, they all travelled by tube. Well, take a look now. There's Rosso's Porsche, Charlie's Range Rover, and top-notch BMWs and Volvos. Holidays over Christmas 2000? Sandy Lane, Barbados (Ross) and Caribbean cruising (Dunstone). It makes you wonder how long they can keep up the 'us against the establishment' ethos.

"Yes, yes," interrupts Dunstone, "Rosso has a Porsche, but he's so un-car-motivated, come on…"

"Yeah, it's an S-reg, it doesn't count," says Ross, giggling.

And the tabloid fascination in his love affair with Ali, sister to Gary Lineker's wife Michelle?

"It's not something I have particularly encouraged, it just happens. I look at it as a bit of a laugh, really… Sometimes journalists come along and see what's going on, yeah, it's curious, but that's… yunno… what it is. And they're incredibly positive about Ali."

And not so positive about his old friend Mr Carling, whose testamonial committee Ross used to chair? Ross's face hardens. "Hmm. I think I will avoid that one at the moment, alright?"

Are they still friends? "Please, that is a story I don't get drawn on."

And then there's the politics. Both men, despite protestations to the contrary, have been increasing their connections with Britain's power elites: Dunstone now sits on the board of the Halifax and helps the Prince's Trust, Ross, according to one friend, networks furiously. He sits on the

Sports Council, socializes with entrepreneurs such as Richer and Johnson, hangs out with sports stars, business stars, agents, media.

These connections are now being parlayed up into political clout. The irony is that, while Dunstone is by instinct a Labour supporter and has been assiduously courted by Peter Mandelson and others, Ross is very firmly on Conservative Central Office's mailing list. Giving to both parties? If they do, it will be done privately. Dunstone abhors business leaders publicly backing parties – it alienates staff and customers, he says – and won't even appear on shows like *Question Time*. He'd just make a prat of himself, he says.

So it is done with discretion, it is done smartly, it is approved of by those who invest in them. And while the results are going their way, while the company is growing fast, and showing good profit, no-one is going to quibble about their lifestyles or their demeanour. There is nothing to quibble about. They are unfailingly courteous. They never rub rivals' noses in it. They never crow. They never over-claim. In fact, Dunstone makes a point of continually under-claiming. They mask their intense competitiveness behind a display of reasoned charm and polite restraint. Maybe it is too polite.

But what about luck?

Sir Alan Sugar leans forward, his face squished up like a wrinkled pickled onion. "There is no luck involved in my business success, I have got to tell you that."

Wagner's new target? Mike Lynch...

Even after all his problems, no-one is writing Dan Wagner off. Many of MAID/Dialog's backers are keeping stakes in Bright Station, which posted an operating loss of £16m for 2000 but promises profit in 2002, just to see what happens. Already there have been little tickles of interest. It was

Wagner who snapped up the technology and programming team from the failed Boo.com e-commerce venture. He's also signed a deal with Intel, the world's biggest chipmaker, which will promote software from two of Bright Station's subsidiaries, SmartLogik (knowledge management) and Sparza (e-commerce). He says his stock is much undervalued now — people don't realise how good a technology play Bright Station could be.

But that surely is down to him?

"It's difficult for me now because there is so much history," says Wagner, staring at the table in front of him, "I can't disappear, but I can step back, and the Bright Station model is structured in that way, the people who run the underlying businesses can step up and be the front people."

Hence Bright Station's highest profile division, SmartLogik software, now has a top executive from Inktomi in charge and David Jeffries, from the National Grid, as chairman. SmartLogik, which operates in similar markets to Autonomy, is a prime contender for flotation or demerger, offering Bright Station shareholders the tantalizing prospect of seeing some cash to compensate for the hard times they have been through.

Yet already there have been whiffs of the old trouble: Wagner briefing journalists that the Intel deal proved a blow for Autonomy; Bright Station press releases claiming that SmartLogik software had outperformed Autonomy's in a customer's test (releases withdrawn); Autonomy chief Mike Lynch making angry ripostes in the press. Ooh, just like old times...

"No, there's no bad feeling on our side, " says Wagner, all innocent. "I don't understand the rationale behind their complaints, we just announced achievements we have made. There's nothing personal between me and Lynch."

In fact, an executive at Autonomy tells me they know just what Wagner's doing – it's what he's always done, he's talking his company up into the same ball park as a far bigger rival. It's infuriating but a lot of the time it works, because Autonomy has to reply in order to ease shareholders' worries. They think Wagner should act more responsibly. Wasn't he on the radio talking up Bright Station's results just days before announcing a loss? Isn't he over-promising and under-performing yet again? But Wagner doesn't see that there is a problem.

So what'll he do if Bright Station flops? Go and run a private company, says Wagner, or live in America. But he doesn't want to. Wife and kid, house in north London's Belsize Park, "just a scooter-ride away" from Highbury where he has a season ticket for the Arsenal. Why would he want to leave?

Others say he works so hard, putting in long hours and surfing the net continuously when he's not working, always fiddling with gadgets, that he could be based anywhere. He shrugs. Bright Station needs my contribution here, he says. "…I'm very plugged in to the tech community, I can identify opportunities that others haven't seen, I've demonstrated that again and again."

And he's right, he has. And there's little doubt he could be very successful again. Everyone wonders, though, whether his personality will keep getting in the way.

But anyway, he says, he loves the people in his company, don't underestimate that, many have been with him for the best part of a decade, he could never leave all that behind. And then he goes off on a rap about his offices, a snitch at £31 per square foot overlooking London's Leicester Square. Yeah, he says, I looked at getting somewhere cheaper, but everywhere is more expensive now and shifting out, getting the wiring they need, it just costs too much. And it's a great location, the programmers love it, working late, seeing the Square, the crowds milling through it.

And you know, he says, sometimes when you walk through Leicester Square, even on a Saturday, and you'll look up, you'll see the lights are on. There are always people here. That's the good thing about this company, whatever happens, it's not just about the boss, it's about more than that, it's about the commitment of its people.

And you realize, whatever luck throws at him, whatever luck he makes, he's hooked. By the summer of 2001, he's changed the company name again ....

acknowledgements

Versions of some of the material in this book first appeared, in different form, in *Management Today*, the *Financial Times*, the *Independent*, the *Observer*, the *Sunday Times*, and *Arena* magazine. I would like to thank all the editors who have commissioned my work, especially Rufus Olins at *Management Today* and Julia Cuthbertson at the *FT*. Thanks too to Harry Borden for the loan of his genius, Rachael Stock at Pearson for being smart enough to put this book together, and Vanessa Nicolson at , who makes me feel lucky every day.